D0734281

Runaway Lives

Tom Smiley

RUNAWAY LIVES

Copyright © 2006 by Tom Smiley

ISBN: 0-9770398-8-9

Published by

LIFEBRIDGE
BOOKS
P.O. BOX 49428
CHARLOTTE, NC 28277

Printed in the United States of America.

DEDICATION

*I am grateful for the undeserved love of God,
the support of an awesome local congregation,
the love of two gracious young men—my sons—and
a family heritage that has provided a good name.
However, it is with genuine humbleness, profound
respect and admiration that I dedicate this book
to my high school sweetheart, my wife of 27
years, my best friend in the world and the most
unselfish person I know. Thank you, Terri.*

CONTENTS

INTRODUCTION

The phone rang.

"Dr. Smiley," said the voice of a concerned friend, "Harris' daughter, Jennifer, is missing."

I've known Harris Wilbanks for several years. His family—and extended family—have been involved in the life of our church for more than four generations.

Troubled, I immediately rushed over and was taken back by the unfolding scene. Law enforcement, media cameras, reporters and curious onlookers were gathering in increasing numbers. There were people in the road handing out "missing person" flyers and local merchants offering free coffee and refreshments.

In the front yard a family friend confided some of her fears and gave me a brief update. Jennifer's well-planned wedding was just days away; it was going to be a huge event, and now the bride had suddenly vanished.

When I found Jennifer's father, Harris, and his wife, Ann, they were both exhausted. I suggested we find a quiet place for some coffee where we could talk. The owner of a nearby restaurant was more than accommodating and offered a private room.

In the eye of the storm, we discussed the situation

regarding Jennifer's disappearance. We prayed, cried, planned and did our best to hold onto hope.

The media blitz moved into overdrive. It was a headline story that riveted the attention of the nation night after night.

"SHE IS ALIVE!"

During those dark hours we rode an emotional roller-coaster. Then, a few days later, a second call came, "Dr. Smiley, Jennifer's been found. She is alive!"

I dressed as quickly as possible. There was barely any traffic on the roads at 2:00 A.M. that morning.

The scene at the home of John, her fiancee, was surreal. Well before daylight, the residence was a sea of people. This time there were more friends, family, reporters and public safety personnel than before. Media tents and the anchors of several national and local news shows were already on location, interviewing the family, bridesmaids and public officials.

A few hours later, Jennifer told the truth about her absence and she boarded a plane home to Georgia.

Two days later, sitting with Jennifer and some family members, we talked, shared some scriptures and prayed for strength and discernment for the coming days.

On May 5, 2005, she requested that I read her statement to the national press. Again, with media lights blazing, I shared her words, which began: "At this time I cannot fully explain what happened last week. I had a host of compelling issues which seemed out of control—issues for which I was unable to address or confine."

Later in the statement was this admission, "I was simply running from myself and from certain fears controlling my life."

In the days that followed, Jennifer explained she was not escaping from her fiancee nor the wedding or marriage. She was running from herself.

The entire episode was not about a runaway bride, rather a runaway life.

LIFE'S UNDERCURRENTS

Growing up in Savannah, Georgia, and being so near the ocean we would often visit and enjoy Tybee Island—a place with a rich heritage and during my young years, an "undiscovered jewel."

My friends and I took great delight in exploring the beach as well as body surfacing and "wop boarding."

On Tybee we were always cautious of the surf since there was the constant potential of rip tides and undercurrents—which could drag a person under and out to sea. They were dangerous, and often deadly.

Now, as a pastor for more than 25 years, there have been numerous times when I have witnessed something quite similar. I have counseled with those whose lives seemed spiraling out of control.

.

IT'S ABOUT YOU!

I began writing this book long before the story of the runaway bride became headlines. It is not about Jennifer, rather about you:

- The mom who rushes everywhere for her kids.
- The dad who thinks working overtime will bring the family closer together.
- The child looking for acceptance and love in all the wrong places.

On these pages we will address the issues which lead to emotional, even physical breakdowns—selfishness, worry, fear, envy, negativity, indecision, discontentment, impatience, temptation and busyness.

Most important, you will learn how to face these problems head on and get your life back on track.

It is my prayer that this practical and timeless advice will help you overcome the emotional undercurrents of life.

– Tom Smiley

CHAPTER 1

DON'T OPEN YOUR UMBRELLA UNTIL IT STARTS RAINING

For God has not given us a spirit of fear,
but of power and of love and of a sound mind.
– 2 TIMOTHY 1:7 NKJV

Concerned, Jane took her beloved elderly father to a psychiatrist, where she told him about her worry over her dad's recent activities.

"He owns this old junk wagon and one horse named Joe," she confided to the the doctor. "He must be getting confused, because each day he drives down the street, yelling, 'Come on Joe! Come on Steve! Come on Sam!'"

The psychiatrist turned to the elderly father and asked, "Well sir, is this true?"

The father replied, "It sure is. If Joe thought he was

pulling the wagon all by himself, he would have quit years ago!"

The psychiatrist took the daughter aside and told her she was worrying needlessly.

"Pulled Apart"

W. H. Auden, the British-American poet, labeled our era as "The age of anxiety."

Worry has been called "the number one mental health disorder in America."

Worry has been called "the number one mental health disorder in America." It can cause insomnia, fatigue, neurosis and physical symptoms which may result in ulcers and cardiovascular problems.

Anxiety is linked to specific panic-inducing situations which can result in dry mouth, shortness of breath, even uncontrollable tears. It has been described as a chronic, vague, never-ending fear: "Something awful is about to happen to wreck everything!"

Others find extreme worry manifested as a apprehension that people are not going to like them or will disapprove based on how they're dressed or the way they talk. This misgiving often causes the "flee" syndrome which compels some sufferers to just up and *leave!* Their only thought is "Stop the world, I want to get off!"

Often, however, we worry unnecessarily over stuff

that never happens. We open up an umbrella and it's not even raining!

The word anxiety literally means: "to be pulled apart."

Throughout the pages of scripture, Jesus thought it was foolish the human race was so worrisome.

If you study what He preached in the "Sermon on the Mount," you will discover Jesus gave more space to the subject of worry than He did to adultery and murder. This truth doesn't mean worry is a greater sin, but indicates that worry and anxiety are prevalent.

WHAT'S WRONG WITH ANXIETY?

When we allow our concerns to dominate our thoughts and actions, the results are often devastating. Here are three reasons:

1. Anxiety magnifies your problems.

A family with a five-year-old went on vacation to a resort unfamiliar to them. Imagine the parents shock when, on arrival, two people on a motor scooter greeted them—and they were totally nude!

The little boy exclaimed, "Mommy, mommy, look! Those people aren't wearing crash helmets!"

The parents' embarrassment and apprehension were totally the opposite of their son's perspective.

Anxiety tends to take the problems and concerns of

13

your life and magnify them way out of proportion.

It reminds me of the agitated patient I heard about who was in a mental hospital. This particular day he was holding his ear close to the wall, listening intently.

The attendant finally approached him.

"Sh!" whispered the patient, beckoning him over.

The attendant pressed his ear to the wall for a long time. "I can't hear a thing," he finally said.

"I know," replied the patient, "It's been like that all day!"

Worry, even among sane people, never accomplishes anything; it has no benefit. It's simply *stewing without doing!*

It is much like a car engine while it's in the "park" gear. The vehicle creates a lot of smoke and noise, but you remain stationary, never going anywhere.

Anxiety cannot alter the past, nor can it control the future. It can only impair your present. As Jesus asks, *"Can all your worries add a single moment to your life? Of course not"* (Matthew 6:27).

Healthy living depends heavily on maintaining the proper perspective—which can be distorted by worry.

2. Anxiety destroys a solid foundation.

Excessive fear and trepidation resemble a jackhammer which pounds away and weakens the very structure of your life. Have you noticed the more you worry, the bigger and more threatening the problem becomes—followed by more mistakes when you address the issue?

As a Christian, you are not an orphan, abandoned in an unfriendly universe. You are a child of the living God who created the world. Scripture shouts: *"Give all your worries and cares to God, for he cares about what happens to you"* (1 Peter 5:7).

> AS A CHRISTIAN, YOU ARE NOT AN ORPHAN, ABANDONED IN AN UNFRIENDLY UNIVERSE.

3. Worry props up suspicion.

Distrust of God can be understandable in the life of a pagan who believes in a jealous, capricious and unpredictable god. But for the one who has learned to call the Almighty "Father," it is beyond my comprehension for that person to distust Him.

The psalmist writes, *"I will remember the works of the Lord; surely I will remember Your wonders of old"* (Psalm 77:11 NKJV).

Place your confidence and trust in the God who has already done such great things for you.

THE PRESCRIPTION FOR WORRY

When you are stressed to the max and riddled with apprehension, let me recommend these three remedies:

First: Count on God's complete care.

The stewardship chairman of a local church was

15

giving his testimony of how the Lord will bless tithing. When he concluded his remarks, he said, "Remember this, ladies and gentlemen, God is always in control."

About that time a small piece of plaster fell on a very wealthy member who had not been listening too closely—or giving to the church! Startled out of his daydreaming, he quickly jumped up and announced, "I'm going to give five dollars a week because of your inspiring talk."

No sooner were the words out of his mouth when an even larger piece of plaster landed on his shoulder. Rising to his feet again, he said, "You know, I'm going to change my giving to *fifty* dollars a week."

Before the pastor could thank him, another chunk of the ceiling came crashing down. Brushing the dust from his hair, the nervous parishioner told the congregation, "I'm going to give five hundred dollars a week!"

Jubilant, the pastor jumped up and exclaimed, "Hit him again, Lord!"

Friend, God *is* always in complete control—and rules every detail of this world, even though we may not understand the "how, when or why."

As God spoke through the prophet Isaiah, *"For as the heavens are higher than the earth, so are My ways higher than your ways, and My thoughts than your thoughts"* (Isaiah 55:9 NKJV).

We worship a God who not only orchestrates the universe, He cares about you as an individual. The psalmist proclaimed, *"The Lord is my shepherd; I have everything I need"* (Psalm 23:1).

As you turn your worry and anxiety over to Him, rest in the assurance the Good Shepherd provides, guides, protects and corrects those in His care.

Isaiah says of God, *"He will feed his flock like a shepherd. He will carry the lambs in his arms, holding them close to his heart. He will gently lead the mother sheep with their young"* (Isaiah 40:11).

The unequaled missionary, Paul, reminds us, *"...this same God who takes care of me will supply all your needs from his glorious riches, which have been given to us in Christ Jesus"* (Philippians 4:19).

> YOU CANNOT EXPECT THE FATHER TO RELIEVE YOUR WORRY AS LONG AS YOU ARE STILL TRYING TO RUN YOUR OWN AFFAIRS.

The only condition God places on meeting your needs is that you invite and allow Him to be the Lord of your life. You cannot expect the Father to relieve your worry as long as you are still trying to run your own affairs.

Second: Accept your Father's love and concern.

Said the robin to the sparrow, "I should really like to know why these anxious human beings rush about and hurry so."

Said the sparrow to the robin, "I think that it must be that they have no Heavenly Father such as cares for you and me."

17

It's true! As Jesus tells us, *"Look at the birds. They don't need to plant or harvest or put food in barns because your heavenly Father feeds them. And you are far more valuable to him than they are"* (Matthew 6:26).

We can accept *any* experience which comes our way, since we know *"all things work together for good to them that love God, to them who are the called according to his purpose"* (Romans 8:28 KJV).

> BY TAKING THE TIME TO DECIDE WHAT IS TRULY IMPORTANT IN YOUR LIFE, YOU CAN LEARN TO PUT FIRST THINGS FIRST.

Joseph's jealous brothers sold him into slavery and meant their actions for evil, *"but God meant it for good"* (Genesis 50:20) —and a great nation was spared.

Joseph received the love, care and concern of the Almighty. So can you!

Three: Establish right priorities.

By taking the time to decide what is truly important in your life you can learn to put first things first.

A speaker at a baccalaureate service challenged the graduates to live a focused, concentrated life. He reminded them what such a choice will accomplish. It will:

- Drive away worry.
- Inspire your vocation.
- Intensify your study.

18

- Purify your life.
- Dominate your well being.

Jesus Himself tells us the benefits of choosing the right priority: *"But seek ye first the kingdom of God, and his righteousness; and all these things shall be added unto you"* (Matthew 6:33 KJV)

Often, we try to escape responsibility for our behavior, but there are seven factors each of us control which have a direct impact on the priorities we choose:

1. We control the clock—choosing how we use each hour.
2. We control our concepts—determining our thoughts and creative imagination.
3. We control our contacts—deciding with whom we will spend most of our time.
4. We control our communication—we are in charge of what we say and how we say it.
5. We control our commitments—determining which concepts, contacts and communications are given priority.
6. We control our causes—selecting our goals.
7. We control our concerns—choosing what we give our attention.

If the compass of your head and heart are fixed on the

right objective, you won't be concerned where your feet are leading you.

Four: Pace yourself.

The future can seem overwhelming when it's viewed in its entirety. But God will provide for you in bite size pieces—one day at a time.

Jesus teaches us that living is a matter of trust. He says, *"...don't worry about tomorrow, for tomorrow will bring its own worries. Today's trouble is enough for today"* (Matthew 6:34).

The wise *prepare* for tomorrow, but the unwise *worry* about tomorrow.

The noted writer Carlisle once observed, "Our main business is not to see what lies dimly in the future, but to do what lies clearly at hand."

Overcoming anxiety is a minute by minute choice. Instead of developing ulcers:

Pray. Acknowledge God's greatness and give Him your adoration and respect. Pray or panic! It's your choice.

Ask. When you are worried, take the matter directly to God. Seek His help and earnestly petition Him. The same Lord who told us to ask, seek, and knock (Matthew 7:7-8) will also answer.

Give thanks. Sometimes we become so wrapped up in

our problems we forget the gracious ways God has worked in the past on our behalf. Every day, let the Lord know how much you appreciate His care.

Ignoring or otherwise trying to eliminate anxiety may result in temporarily winning the battle but ultimately losing the war. You will discover that dealing with your worry head-on will cause you to ask countless questions and give you insight into yourself.

If you stress out over health, marriage, children and vocational issues, learn to deal with them *daily.* Otherwise, you may experience more than a rain storm. Thankfully, it's a situation you can avoid.

Rejoice in the fact, *"You can throw the whole weight of your anxieties upon him, for you are his personal concern"* (1 Peter 5:7 PT).

Why run away from your problems when you have a loving Father who is waiting to share His love and concern?

Chapter 2

If You're Burning the Candle at Both Ends, You Aren't as Bright as You Think You Are!

*It is senseless for you to work so hard
from early morning until late at night, fearing
you will starve to death; for God wants
his loved ones to get their proper rest.*

— Psalm 127:2 LB

In a *Peanuts* comic strip there was a conversation between Lucy and Charley Brown.

Lucy said that life is like a lounge chair on your deck: "Some place it so they can see where they are going.

23

Some place it so they can see where they have been."

Charley Brown replied, "I can't even get mine unfolded!"

Mistakenly, people equate *busyness* as a status symbol for success. A widely accepted assumption is that anyone who is always active must be an achiever. The truth is, being over-scheduled, over-committed and weary does not guarantee success.

If the following statements describe you, then you're too busy:

- I constantly feel in a hurry.
- My "to do" list is always long.
- I use my day off to complete unfinished work.
- I feel guilty when I relax.
- My family refers to me "as occupant."

Why is busyness such a big deal? If we become so distracted by the hustle and bustle of our daily activities, we will settle for mediocrity.

God is interested in your rest and recreation. He desires for you to enjoy a balanced life and doesn't want you to *constantly* labor.

Our existence can become so complicated, so cluttered, so hectic that we become inundated. This undercurrent can be devastating to your career, family and future.

A Bible scholar once said: "Busyness is not *of* the devil. Busyness *is* the devil."

Look at this contemporary warning written thousands of years ago: *"It is senseless for you to work so hard from early morning until late at night, fearing you will starve to death; for God wants his loved ones to get their proper rest"* (Psalm 127:2 LB).

UNWIND "GOD'S WAY

How do you relax in a fast-paced, computer age that is whizzing by at the speed of light? Let me recommend these six steps:

Step one: Realize your worth to the Almighty.

Many people over-extend themselves physically because they confuse their work with their worth. They think, "If I work hard and achieve much, I must also be worth much." Wrong!

Jesus tells us, *"...real life is not measured by how much we own"* (Luke 12:15).

You are already a valued treasure to the Lord. As scripture declares, *"In his goodness he chose to make us his own children by giving us his true word. And we, out of all creation, became his choice*

> MANY PEOPLE OVER-EXTEND THEMSELVES PHYSICALLY BECAUSE THEY CONFUSE THEIR WORK WITH THEIR WORTH.

25

possession" (James 1:18).

You don't need to demonstrate the world's definition of success to be happy—or prove your significance to others by what you have accumulated. The only measure which matters is your value to the Creator.

Step two: Take pleasure in life as you go.

If you are not careful you can become so preoccupied with wanting more that you fail to enjoy what you have. Take this advice from King Solomon:*"And people should eat and drink and enjoy the fruits of their labor, for these are gifts from God"* (Ecclesiastes 3:13).

Solomon also says, *"Then I observed that most people are motivated to success by their envy of their neighbors. But this, too, is meaningless, like chasing the wind"* (Ecclesiastes 4:4).

The wise person enjoys life as he goes—taking pleasure in every sunrise and delighting in every day.

Step three: Choose eternal values.

Life is more than a nine to five job and putting aside a nest egg for a rainy day. Our priorities should reflect the fact our time here is temporary—it is only preparation for eternity.

Here is specific counsel on this subject from the Son of God: *"Don't store up treasures here on earth, where they can be eaten by moths and get rusty, and where thieves break in and steal. Store your treasures in heaven, where they will never become moth-eaten or rusty and where they will be safe from thieves. Wherever your treasure is, there your heart and thoughts will also be"* (Matthew 6:19-21).

Remember to seek His kingdom *first*, then attend to earthly matters.

Step four: Fight materialism.

Often, our lack of time is tied to our hurry to become rich—to feed our greed!

This principle is established in God's Word: *"A faithful man will abound with blessings, but he who makes haste to be rich will not go unpunished"* (Proverbs 28:20 NASB).

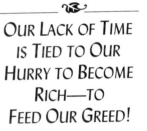

OUR LACK OF TIME IS TIED TO OUR HURRY TO BECOME RICH—TO FEED OUR GREED!

Materialistic people are rarely patient—they are consumed with acquiring more.

By waging a personal war against accumulating "things" and discarding what is not really necessary, you might be surprised how much time is freed up for you to enjoy what you already possess.

An expert on time management advises you may lose money, but you can always earn more. You may lose your possessions, yet you can always acquire new ones. However, time is a non-renewable commodity. If you squander your minutes and hours, they are lost forever.

27

Step five: Limit your labor.

On Tuesday, pastor John received an irate call from a parishioner, frustrated she could not contact him the day before. "Well," he politely explained, "Monday is my day off."

The lady bluntly told him, "The devil doesn't take a day off."

The pastor replied, "Yes, and if I didn't, I'd be just like him!"

Everyone needs a time of refreshing. God set the rules in His Word: *"Six days a week are set apart for your daily duties and regular work, but the seventh day is a day of rest dedicated to the Lord your God. On that day no one in your household may do any kind of work. This includes you, your sons and daughters, your male and female servants, your livestock, and any foreigners living among you"* (Exodus 20:9-10).

An ancient proverb says, "Too many irons in the fire smothers the flame."

Relax! Take a break!

Step six: Practice solitude.

One of the most influential books I ever read was *The Practice of the Presence of God* by Brother Lawrence. I learned the principle of guarding my heart with times of quiet. If you don't "pull apart" you will "come apart!"

Follow the example of Jesus: *"Then, because so*

many people were coming and going that they did not even have a chance to eat, he said to them, 'Come with me by yourselves to a quiet place and get some rest'" (Mark 6:31 NIV).

Life must be lived in a rhythm of engagement and withdrawal, engagement and withdrawal. It's the only way to recharge your tired batteries.

When you learn the proper way to burn the candle, you'll find all the light needed for your journey.

CHAPTER 3

WHICH BRIDGE TO BURN, WHICH BRIDGE TO CROSS

*There is a path before each person
that seems right, but it ends in death.*

– PROVERBS 14:12

The undercurrent of poor decision-making can be especially damaging. Your life can be changed forever by just one wrong choice. Before you think no bridge should ever be "burned," it may be better for some decisions to be left behind forever.

There are two sides to a sheet of flypaper—and it makes a big difference to the fly which side he chooses!

A wise man once said, "We make our decisions, then our decisions make us."

DISCOVERING SOUND GUIDANCE

Methods vary regarding how people make their choices. Here are a few options I've observed people use:

- Put out a fleece.
- Flip a coin or draw straws.
- Delegate the decision making to others.
- Flounder in indecision.

In speaking about the choices of his friends, the humorist Will Rogers wryly commented, "Some of my friends are for it, some of my friends are against it, and I'm for my friends!"

There's a more reliable method to making practical, common-sense choices. Consider these three factors:

First: Recognize your limitations.

We foolishly think we are able to make competent choices without God's help. We reason, "If the Lord gave me a brain, why is it so important for me to ask Him for help in making decisions?"

The answer becomes obvious when you understand that God knows you better than you know yourself. It is imperative to admit your personal limitations.

Remember: *"There is a path before each person that seems right, but it ends in death"* (Proverbs 14:12).

Second: Ask in faith for God's guidance.

Receiving discernment from the Lord involves:

- Our asking Him.
- Our asking Him with the right motivation.
- Our asking and waiting on Him.

While Christian counseling is helpful, don't fail to open the pages of God's Word to discover guidance you need. For example: *"If you need wisdom—if you want to know what God wants you to do–ask him, and he will gladly tell you. He will not resent your asking. But when you ask him, be sure that you really expect him to answer, for a doubtful mind is as unsettled as a wave of the sea that is driven and tossed by the wind. People like that should not expect to receive anything from the Lord"* (James 1:5-7).

ARE YOU EXPECTING YOUR FATHER'S SOLUTION?

Are you expecting your Father's solution?

Third: Listen for God's response.

How does the Lord communicate with His children?

- God speaks through His Word.
- God speaks through godly teachers.
- God speaks through circumstances.
- God speaks through pain and disappointment.

The challenge for us is learning to hear Him! Even in this twenty-first century, Job's words still ring true, *"But God speaks again and again, though people do not recognize it"* (Job 33:14).

This failure involves a spiritual battle. As Paul writes, *"For the flesh lusts against the spirit, and the spirit against the flesh; and these are contrary to one another, so that you do not do the things that you wish"* (Galatians 5:17 NKJV).

GET ON THE RIGHT ROAD

Never question the path on which the Lord is leading you until you reach the end of your journey. *"Your road led through the sea, your pathway through the mighty waters—a pathway no one knew was there!"* (Psalm 77:19).

Avoid making hasty decisions about an unfinished plan. Stay the course by placing your total faith and confidence in God. *"Trust in the Lord with all your heart and lean not on your own understanding; in all your ways acknowledge him, and he will make your paths straight"* (Proverbs 3:5-6 NIV).

Don't expect God to reveal His will for you tomorrow until you practice His will today.

CHAPTER 4

NEVER MISMANAGE A HURT

**Surely resentment destroys the
fool, and jealousy kills the simple.**

– JOB 5:2

Whoever said "Sticks and stones can break my bones but words can never hurt me," knew very little about the scars and pains emotional hurts create.

Jesus said, *"In this world you will have trouble. But take heart! I have overcome the world"* (John 16:33 NIV).

I am convinced some of the "trouble" Jesus predicted we would experience is that of being emotionally injured!

None of us are immune, and the deepest, most lasting wounds, may come from the people we are closest to!

It's only natural to search for answers.

What Won't Work

Before we discuss the process of healing, let me suggest three remedies to avoid:

1. Ignoring your hurt.

Pretending the distress isn't there or didn't happen will not bring closure.

> **PRETENDING THE DISTRESS ISN'T THERE OR DIDN'T HAPPEN WILL NOT BRING CLOSURE.**

Perhaps your experience mirrors what the psalmist endured: *"But as I stood there silently the turmoil within me grew to the bursting point. The more I mused, the hotter the fires inside. Then at last I spoke, and pled with God"* (Psalm 39:2-3 LB).

Don't deny the emotional pain or minimize the anguish you are feeling. Also, do not procrastinate getting into the Word and perhaps seeking professional Christian counsel.

Just ignoring the situation never works!

2. Running from your hurt.

When problems engulf us, there is a huge temptation to start running—even if we don't have the foggiest notion where we're headed! We feel like David when he daydreamed: *"Oh, how I wish I had wings like a dove; then I would fly away and rest! How quickly I would escape—far away from this wild storm of hatred"* (Psalm 55:6,8).

But where should we go? The sidewalks of life are littered with wounded individuals who use these deadly escape routes:

- Entertainment—seeking to bury our lives in pleasure to escape from reality.
- Drugs—searching for a state of euphoria, only to be trapped into dependency.
- Alcoholism—turning to the bottle as a mind-numbing crutch.
- Workaholism—avoiding issues by totally absorbing your time and energy in your career.

A psychologist friend once told me, "The most serious problem which results from running from your pain is: *nothing ever changes."*

The truth remains. Whatever wound you are camouflaging—covering up with a smile or wearing under a mask— will only escalate over time and become more and more destructive.

3. Rehearsing your hurt.

Clara Barton, founder of the American Red Cross,

was reminded one day of a vicious act someone had inflicted on her years before. But she reacted as if she had never even heard of the incident. "Don't you remember?" her friend inquired.

"No," came Barton's reply, "I distinctly remember forgetting it."

Friendships are *dependant* on our intentional lapse of memory.

Scripture reminds us how important forgetting a hurt is to a meaningful relationship: *"Surely resentment destroys the fool, and jealousy kills the simple"* (Job 5:2).

Mulling over and over the issue never brings finality. *"You will keep your friends if you forgive them, but you will lose your friends if you keep talking about what they did wrong"* (Proverbs 17:9 CEV).

GETTING WELL

Regardless of how deep the pain you feel, there is an escape route from your anguish.

First: Seek healing over revenge.

It doesn't pay to retaliate. If there is a score to be settled, let the action be taken by the Lord, not you.

Paul counsels: *"Do not repay anyone evil for evil. Be careful to do what is right in the eyes of everybody. Do not take revenge, my friends, but leave room for God's wrath, for it is written: 'It is mine to avenge; I will repay,' says the Lord"* (Romans 12:17,19 NIV).

Today, decide between revenge or release.

Second: Use God's restoration keys.

The days may be dark, yet as long as you are drawing a breath, you can start over. The Lord has given us keys which will open the door to renewal.

> THE DAYS MAY BE DARK, YET AS LONG AS YOU ARE DRAWING A BREATH, YOU CAN START OVER.

The key of hope.

Through the eyes of belief and expectation, see yourself returning to a place of peace. *"So I pray that God, who gives you hope, will keep you happy and full of peace as you believe in him. May you overflow with hope through the power of the Holy Spirit"* (Romans 15:13).

The key of love.

You are not alone. There are people in your life who cherish you—regardless of what has transpired. Don't close the door on their genuine affection. *"And may the Lord make your love grow and overflow to each other and to everyone else, just as our love overflows toward you"* (1 Thessalonians 3:12).

The key of joy.

Don't become so absorbed in self-pity that you can't

find anything to smile about. Jesus says, *"You haven't done this before. Ask, using my name, and you will receive, and you will have abundant joy"* (John 16:24).

**In the depths of your desperation,
you have searched in vain for solutions.
Isn't it time to try God's way?**

CHAPTER 5

THE FEAR FACTOR

For God has not given us a spirit of fear and
timidity, but of power, love, and self-discipline.
– 2 TIMOTHY 1:7

Peope everywhere are tormented by fear—a
dangerous and deadly undercurrent of life. If left
unchallenged, it will rob you of vitality, enthusiasm,
anticipation and progress.

If you were asked to list your three greatest fears,
what would they be? And what have you done to deal
with these "monsters" which seem to loom larger than
life?

What may begin as a mild uneasiness, can suddenly
turn into hysteria and panic. This "anticipated danger"
becomes a thief who steals your dreams and drains your
energy.

Friend, the Lord doesn't want you to waste your
talents; He intends for you to use them for His glory.
That's why you *must* get a handle on your fear.

THE BITTER FRUIT OF FEAR

When you allow this seed to take root, it will grow into a twisted tree which will produce an unwanted harvest. *Here is what you can expect:*

Potential paralyzed.

Have you ever thought, "Wow! I'd love to do that," or, "I've dreamed of this" but you were too scared to venture out of your comfort zone?

> *IT LIMITS AND IMMOBILIZES— KEEPING YOU FROM ALL GOD DESIRES YOU TO BE.*

That's what fear does. It limits and immobilizes—keeping you from all God desires you to be. It causes you to miss opportunities, to pull back and keep your dreams locked in a box.

The issue affects every person—including believers.

Just after the crucifixion of Jesus, the disciples were huddled together in a room with the doors bolted, for fear of the Jewish authorities (John 20:19).

I find it interesting that when you lock a door it's usually from the inside—it is self-imposed. No one is confining you, rather you make the decision for yourself.

Relationships destroyed.

What we are discussing is not a new phenomena. Fear

reared its ugly head just after creation. After Adam and Eve disobeyed God, they covered themselves and went into hiding in the garden of Eden—breaking their relationship with the Father.

Of course, God knew exactly where Adam was; yet, He asked him, "Where are you?"

Adam replied, *"I heard you, so I hid. I was afraid..."* (Genesis 3:10).

Today, fear still plays a pivotal role in relationships. Talk to any psychologist and he will tell you how lives are negatively affected by:

- The fear of rejection.
- The fear of commitment.
- The fear of not living up to expectations.
- The fear of intimacy.

In addition, friendships can be permanently damaged when fear prevents honesty—building walls instead of bridges.

Happiness hindered.

It is totally impossible to be afraid and joyful at the same time!

You only need to glance at a person to know how they are reacting to a situation. When the tide of uncertainty rises, it's obvious. You can see the furrowed brow, the tightened jaw, the terror-filled eyes.

In the words of Solomon, *"Worry can rob you of happiness..."* (Proverbs 12:25 TEV).

Success sabotaged.

One of the primary reasons people won't risk changing directions in life or starting a new business is because their fear of failure far outweighs their desire to succeed.

They stress, "What will my friends think of me if I don't make it?"

So instead of dreaming and becoming creative, their productive energies are zapped by thoughts of what "might" go wrong. They are like David, who admitted, *"I am worn out by my worries"* (Psalm12:25 TEV).

Fear creates what it fears.

PERHAPS YOU HAVE SAID TO YOURSELF, "I WAS AFRAID THAT WAS GOING TO HAPPEN."

Perhaps you have said to yourself, "I was afraid that was going to happen."

Guess what! You have just set yourself up for failure.

What we think about is often what we receive. For example:

- Your fear of illness causes you to focus on becoming sick—and before you know it, you are!
- Your fear of disappointing someone keeps you

from acting naturally and you end up letting
them down anyway.

- The fear of not being attractive makes certain
  women wear too much makeup and they look
  hard and artificial.
- The fear of poverty causes many to make risky
  investments—losing what little money they
  had.
- The fear of growing old results in people aging
  prematurely.

Job said to his friends, *"What I always feared has
happened to me. What I dreaded has come to be"* (Job
3:25).

Be careful what you fear!

REAL OR IMAGINED?

According to pediatric studies, there are only two
basic fears we are born with: (1) the fear of falling and
(2) the fear of loud noises.

Consequently, our other fears are picked up along
life's journey.

Here's the good news! If only two fears were inborn
in you as an infant, all others you have acquired can be
unlearned.

Why should we worry unnecessarily when most of
what we are anxious about never comes to pass?

One research study revealed:

- 40% of fears focus on future events which never take place.
- 30% concern the past—things you can never change.
- 12% are needless fears concerning a person's health—which never materialize.
- 10% are petty fears which really aren't even worth agonizing over.

The remaining 8% are legitimate concerns which we can take appropriate action against.

Sure, there are "healthy" fears we instill in our children—such as learning not to touch a hot stove or walking into traffic—but most of the things of which we are afraid are an exercise in futility.

DIVINE ANTIDOTES FOR FEAR

There's no reason to spend your years caught in a web of worry. Let me give you three sure-fire solutions:

Fill your heart with divine truth.

Most fears are the result of false evidence appearing real.

If a person walks into a room with a play gun and says, "This is a robbery!" even though it may be an April

Fools prank, you experience a moment of sheer terror.

We can't base our life on faulty assumptions or misconceptions. Rather, we must challenge every fear with the truth—as quickly as possible. The words of Jesus are still relevant: *"...you will know the truth, and the truth will set you free"* (John 8:32).

> WE BECOME LIBERATED BY SHINING THE SPOTLIGHT OF REALITY ON EVERY SITUATION.

We become liberated by shining the spotlight of reality on every situation. As Paul writes, *"In the full light of God's truth, we live"* (2 Corinthians 4:2 TEV).

Fill your heart with divine love.

When anger and resentment are replaced with God's love, fear is literally pushed out. Why? Because, *"Love contains no fear—indeed fully-developed love expels every particle of fear, for fear always contains some of the torture of feeling guilty"* (1 John 4:18 PT).

When you fully understand how much the Lord cares for His children, it will allow you to stop fearing the rejection of other people. It is the ultimate satisfaction to experience His unconditional love.

Much of our anxiety is self-centered, and when our attention is only on *us*, we become anxious and afraid.

However, drastic changes occur when love begins to dominate and we focus on the needs of others.

Fill your life with divine faith.

Your adversary, Satan, is a master at scare tactics. He likes nothing more than to see you cowering in a corner, worried over what he has planted in your mind.

How do we build an effective barrier against his attacks? Through an armor of faith. Scripture tells us, *"Above all, be sure to take faith as your shield, for it can quench every burning missile that the enemy hurls at you"* (Ephesians 6:16 PT).

Do you believe—*really* believe—God can supernaturally intervene on your behalf?

- Faith produces agreement—fear produces discord.
- Faith advances—fear retreats.
- Faith expects the best—fear expects the worst.
- Faith is action—fear is paralysis.
- Faith is day—fear is night
- Faith gives—fear takes.
- Faith creates peace—fear creates tension.

It takes total belief to move against your feelings; yet, move is what the Lord asks you to do—because your emotions are not always a reliable barometer.

As yourself this question, "Is there one area in my life

where I need to take a step of faith, but fear holds me hostage?"

- Is it making a career move?
- Is it committing to marriage?
- Is it accepting Christ?
- Is it rededicating your life?
- Is it joining a church?
- Is it attending a small group for Bible study?

By faith, make the bold decision to face your fear head on. The rewards far outweigh any risks. As the Word declares, *"...without faith it is impossible to please God, because anyone who comes to him must believe that he exists and that he rewards those who earnestly seek him"* (Hebrews 11:6 NIV).

Great fear trembles in the presence of great faith.

CHAPTER 6

DON'T BE FRIGHTENED OF THE FUTURE!

*Surely goodness and love will follow
me all the days of my life and I will dwell
in the house of the Lord forever.*
– PSALM 23:6 NIV

From time to time, all of us have questions concerning our future—only to be surprised at what we discover.

I'm reminded of the tale of the frog who visited a fortune teller trying to get an insight into his future. She gazed intently into the crystal ball and told the frog: "You are going to meet a beautiful young woman. From the moment she sets her eyes on you she will have an insatiable desire to know everything about you. She will be compelled to get close to you—and you will fascinate her."

Excited, the frog asked, "Where am I? At a single's party?"

"No," replied the fortune teller, "in a biology class!"

51

SO MUCH FOR THE "EXPERTS"

People love to predict the future, but history shows it's not an exact science. For example:

- "Everything that can be invented has been invented."– Charles H. Duell, Commissioner, U.S. Office of Patents, 1899.

- "Airplanes are interesting toys, but of no military value."– Maréchal Ferdinand Foch, Professor of Strategy, Ecole Supérieure de Guerre, 1911.

- "Theoretically, television may be feasible, but I consider it an impossibility—a development which we should waste little time dreaming about." – Lee de Forest, inventor of the cathode ray tube, 1926.

- "Stocks have reached what looks like a permanently high plateau." – Irving Fisher, Professor of Economics, Yale University, October 16, 1929.

- "Whatever happens, the U.S. Navy is not going to be caught napping." Frank Knox,

U.S. Secretary of the Navy, December 4,
1941.

- "I think there is a world market for about five
  computers." – Thomas J. Watson, chairman
  of the board of IBM, 1943.

- "With over 50 foreign cars already on sale
  here, the Japanese auto industry isn't likely
  to carve out a big slice of the U.S. market."
  – *Business Week,* 1958.

- "We don't like their sound. Groups of guitars
  are on the way out." – Decca Recording
  Company executive rejecting the Beatles,
  1962.

As many "experts" have learned, getting a grip on the
future can be as tough as "nailing Jell-O to the wall!"

YOU CAN KNOW TOMORROW

If you want to face the days ahead with confidence,
start claiming the promises found in God's Word—His
covenant with you. When your Heavenly Father makes
a prediction it's not mere guesswork. Why? Because He
is Alpha and Omega, and knows the beginning from the
end.

This same God is deeply concerned over your well being and holds your future in His hands.

Someone is watching over you.

God didn't forget about Paul when he was thrown into prison. It was while he was confined to a cell he was inspired to write much of what we now call the New Testament.

The Lord knew exactly where Joseph was when his brothers sold him into slavery. They meant to harm him, but God elevated Joseph into a position of authority and power to provide for those who had treated him so badly.

GOD KNOWS WHERE YOU ARE AT THIS VERY MOMENT.

When Jesus was nailed to the cross, Satan thought he had scuttled God's great plan of redemption. Yet the Father was always looking after His Son—and I'm sure you have read the rest of the story! The Bible tells us, *"The Lord watches over all who love him, but all the wicked he will destroy"* (Psalm 145:20 NIV).

God knows where you are at this very moment.

Your Father cares about the details of your life.

The same God who counts every hair on your head is also concerned with where you will be tomorrow. David said, *"You chart the path ahead of me and tell me where to stop and rest. Every moment you know where I am"* (Psalm 139:3).

Since the Almighty has a blueprint of your destiny, you don't need to be afraid of the unknown. You can say with authority, *"The Lord will work out his plans for my life..."* (Psalm 138:8). And you can rest assured He will fulfill His promise, *"I will guide you along the best pathway for your life. I will advise you and watch over you"* (Psalm 32:8).

God's grace continues to work in you.

The "born again" experience is not self-produced. The Word tells us, *"For it is by grace you have been saved, through faith—and this not from yourselves, it is the gift of God"* (Ephesians 2:8 NIV).

This same amazing grace is still at work, challenging you to grow and develop—molding and shaping your future.

There is a brighter tomorrow on the horizon.

Your body was not designed to last on this earth forever. The Bible says, *"Seventy years are given to us! Some may even reach eighty..."* (Psalm 90:10)—and modern science is trying to stretch it even further.

However, the grave is not our final resting place. You will spend eternity in one of two places—with Christ in the city not made with hands or with the devil in outer darkness. *"Don't envy sinners, but always continue to fear the Lord. For surely you have a future ahead of you; your hope will not be disappointed"* (Proverbs 23:17-18).

As a believer, you are headed for a better destination, *"For we know that when this earthly tent we live in is taken down—when we die and leave these bodies—we will have a home in heaven, an eternal body made for us by God himself and not by human hands"* (2 Corinthians 5:1).

I pray you have made preparations for that great day!

You're in Good Hands!

Consider whose hands you are in!

- A rod in my hands might keep me from stumbling; a rod in Moses' hands will part the waters.
- A sling in my hands is a child's toy; a sling in David's hands will fell a mighty warrior.
- A basketball in my hands is worth $20; a basketball in Michael Jordan's hands is worth about $33 million.
- A baseball in my hands is worth $5; a baseball in Alex Rodriguez's hands is valued at about $250 million.
- A tennis racquet in my hands may be worth $95; a tennis racquet in Pete Sampras' hands is worth a Wimbledon championship.

■ A golf club in my hands is absolutely worthless;
    a golf club in Tiger Woods' hands is priceless.

It all depends on whose hands!

If you long for comfort to ease a troubled heart, place your worries and fears about tomorrow in His nail-scarred hands. The Lord will exchange them for hope and will bless you with the desire of your heart.

As Ralph Waldo Emerson observed, "All I have seen teaches me to trust the Creator for all I have not seen!"

Sometimes the Lord calms the storm.
Sometimes He lets the storm rage and calms His
child. No matter which He chooses for you,
you no longer have to fear the future!

CHAPTER 7

WHEN YOU ARE GREEN WITH ENVY, YOU ARE RIPE FOR TROUBLE

*What causes fights and quarrels
among you? Don't they come from your
desires that battle within you?*
— JAMES 4:1 NIV

The devil was doing his best to lead a certain priest into sin. He tried everything in the book—lust, money, all to no avail. The priest withstood every temptation *except one!*

Finally, Satan whispered in his ear, "Did you hear that your younger brother has surpassed you and has just been named a Cardinal?"

Jealousy is an ugly word. It has overtones of selfishness, suspicion, distrust; it implies a hideous

59

resentment, or even hostility, toward other people because they enjoy some advantage over you.

In *Othello*, Shakespeare refers to jealousy as "the green-eyed monster."

Today some mistakenly call it "having a competitive spirit;" yet, according to the Bible, it is far more harmful: *"An angry person is dangerous, but a jealous person is even worse"* (Proverbs 27:4 CEV).

Scripture is filled with accounts of the damaging effects of envy:

- The first sons born to Adam and Eve were not only sibling rivals, Cain killed Abel because of envy (Genesis 4).
- Joseph was sold into slavery by his jealous brothers (Genesis 37).
- King Saul grew envious of the shepherd boy, David, because of his popularity in killing Goliath (1 Samuel 18).
- The pharisees and religious leaders turned Jesus over to the authorities because of their jealousy (Mark 15).

Envy is a cancer which comes from the devil's hell. Remember, it was Lucifer who said he wanted to be like God—and his rivalry resulted in him being kicked out of heaven.

THE PROBLEMS WITH ENVY

Jealousy is not some petty nuisance or minor life weakness. Envy:

- Is possessive.
- Is demanding.
- Stifles freedom and individuality.
- Degrades and demeans.
- Breeds tension and discord.
- Destroys happiness.
- Leads to other sins.

These are only a few of the problems it causes. Let's look at four specific dangers:

1. Envy distracts you from your life's purpose.

Recognize the risk of watching the actions of others, wishing, "If only I had what they have—their money, their gifts, their abilities."

Jesus has strong words for those who allow their attention to be diverted from their life mission. He says, *"Anyone who lets himself be distracted from the work I plan for him is not fit for the Kingdom of God"* (Luke 9:62 LB).

Just as an Olympic medal winner keeps his eyes straight ahead when he is running the race, we too must stay focused on the prize.

2. Envy causes conflict in every relationship.

As children we used to play, "King of the Hill."

The rules were simple: find a mound of dirt and have several kids try to get to the top. The one who reaches the summit first is named "king" until someone pushes him aside and becomes his successor.

Unfortunately, many adults are playing the same game today—in a much more subtle way.

Some play King of the Hill, flaunting the material things they purchase, or perhaps making sure others see the color of their credit card.

Even bumper stickers have an undertone of envy and pride: "My Child is an Honor Student at Eastside Elementary School."

CONFLICT ALWAYS RESULTS WHEN WE ATTEMPT TO GET "ONE UP" ON SOMEONE ELSE.

A friend of mine swears he saw one that read, "My Son was Inmate of the Month at Riedsville State Prison."

Conflict always results when we attempt to get "one up" on someone else. As James asks, *"What causes fights and quarrels among you? Don't they come from your desires that battle within you?"* (James 4:1 NIV).

When I covet what you have, there will always be discord.

3. Envy will make you miserable.

A jealous spirit is worse than any disease your

physical body may endure. King Solomon wrote, *"A heart at peace gives life to the body, but envy rots the bones"* (Proverbs 14:30 NIV).

It "eats away" at your core until you are stripped of everything worthwhile and decent.

Whose bones does envy rot? The person who is envious—not the object of their resentment.

The apostle Paul spoke of those who suppress the truth and live according to their sinful behavior: *"They have become filled with every kind of wickedness, evil, greed and depravity. They are full of envy, murder, strife, deceit and malice. They are gossips, slanderers, God-haters, insolent, arrogant and boastful; they invent ways of doing evil; they disobey their parents; they are senseless, faithless, heartless, ruthless. Although they know God's righteous decree that those who do such things deserve death, they not only continue to do these very things but also approve of those who practice them"* (Romans 1:29-32 NIV).

That's quite a list!

SEVEN STEPS TO SLAYING THE GREEN-EYED MONSTER

You may say, "I know the problem, but what is the solution? How do I conquer the spirit of envy?

Since jealousy is too dangerous to be ignored, let me recommend these steps:

1. Admit your jealousy.

Most people find it easier to admit almost *any* sin than to confess to envy. They will acknowledge their personal mistakes or poor judgement, but there aren't many who are quick to acknowledge this flaw.

The reason? When you confess jealousy, it reveals the pettiness in your own heart.

Why not get the problem out in the open so you can bury it once and for all. Take the counsel of James the Apostle as translated in the New Jerusalem Bible, *"But if at heart you have the bitterness of jealousy, or selfish ambition, don't be boastful or hide the truth with lies"* (James 3:14).

Admit it!

2. Do not minimize the problem.

Jealousy attacks people of every age, culture and economic level. It's not an insignificant issue, but an infection with grave consequences: *"For wherever there is jealousy and selfish ambition, there you will find disorder and every kind of evil"* (James 3:16).

According to scripture, an envious person keeps bad company—equated with adulterers and idolaters. Paul

> ACCORDING TO SCRIPTURE, AN ENVIOUS PERSON KEEPS BAD COMPANY— EQUATED WITH ADULTERERS AND IDOLATERS.

writes, *"The acts of the sinful nature are obvious: sexual immorality, impurity and debauchery; idolatry and witchcraft; hatred, discord, jealousy, fits of rage, selfish ambition, dissensions, factions"* (Galatians 5:19-20 NIV).

Most of us would never become involved with witchcraft; yet, we allow jealousy to creep into our heart and spirit. In God's sight there is no difference.

3. Refuse to compare yourself to others.

Soon after the resurrection, Jesus was talking with Peter and John and told Peter, "You are going to die a very violent death in service to Me."

That news didn't seem to upset Peter. However, he looked at John and asked the Lord, "Well, how is *he* going to die?"

Jesus answered, *"...what is that to you?"* (John 12:23). In other words, "It's none of your business! Don't worry over what will happen to John. I have a plan for *your* life and that's all you need to be concerned with."

If you measure your life against another person, you become discouraged—thinking either, "They are so much better than me," or "I can do it best."

Don't draw a comparison between yourself and the person to your left or right. The Bible tells us, *"Let everyone be sure to do his very best for then he will have the personal satisfaction of work done well, and won't need to compare himself with someone else"* (Galatians 6:4 LB).

4. Recognize your uniqueness.

Dr. Frank Harrington, the noted preacher, was one of my beloved professors in seminary.

While speaking on the subject of personal distinctiveness, he told us of the time he attended a golf tournament and actually enjoyed a conversation with Jack Nicklaus.

Some of his friends were so impressed with his good fortune, they said to Dr. Harrington, "How did it feel to rub elbows with the greatest golfer in the world?"

"It was okay," replied the professor.

"Just okay?" they responded.

Harrington wryly commented, "Jack Nicklaus may be the greatest golfer in the world, but can he preach?"

You are unique! As David expressed, *"You* [God] *created every part of me; you put me together in my mother's womb"* (Psalm 139:13 TEV). In other words, you have "designer genes."

The psalmist added, *"You saw me before I was born and scheduled every day of my life before I began to breathe"* (Psalm 139:15 LB).

When you understand the Lord has a "customized" plan for your entire life, you will finally see the foolishness of envy. No longer will you think, "I wish God had made me taller or shorter—bigger or smaller, or smarter."

You are one of a kind—formed intentionally. Oh, you may not fathom the incredible wonder of your creation or even like the result; nevertheless, the Lord made you for a reason, with the talents you do or do not possess.

Envy is a human expression of inferiority and is based on insecurity. When you are jealous because of what others have or who others are, you are really criticizing God for not making you different.

> *ENVY IS A HUMAN EXPRESSION OF INFERIORITY AND IS BASED ON INSECURITY.*

The issue is not becoming what you *aren't* but becoming fully what God has designed you to be. He has an agenda for your life which is tailor-made exclusively for you—not anyone else. It is yours alone.

5. Rejoice in what you do have.

A favorite saying of an elderly friend goes like this, "It's not what you lost that matters. It is what you have left that counts."

Millions attempt to find happiness by following these two myths: (1) "I need to be like you," and (2) "I need to have *more* than you."

When you buy into these two fallacies, you will be consumed by the desire to acquire. What a contrast from the words of Jesus, who said, *"...one's life does not consist in the abundance of the things he possesses"* (Luke 12:15 NKJV).

The first rule in the School of Contentment is to know, "I already have more than I deserve, so I don't need another thing." According to a principle established in God's Word, *"Enjoy what you have rather than desiring what you don't have. Just dreaming about nice things is meaningless; it is like chasing the wind"* (Ecclesiastes 6:9).

Paul expressed it this way, *"I have learned how to get along happily whether I have much or little"* (Philippians 4:11). He discovered how to be content. It is not a natural behavior but an acquired skill.

Envy results when I resent God's goodness in other's lives while ignoring God's goodness in mine.

Delight in what you have *left*, never in what you have *lost*.

6. Respond to others in love.

A wise pastor once reminded me of this truth, "You will know when two people are truly companions. When one has a sorrow, it is halved; and when one has a joy, it is doubled."

Speaking of envy, there are two distinct behaviors between a "carnal man" and "spiritual man." The *flesh* provokes you to laugh when people fail and cry when they succeed. However, when love permeates your heart, you will, *"Rejoice with those who rejoice, weep with those who weep"* (Romans 12:15).

This sentiment is possible because *"love does not*

envy" (1 Corinthians 13:14).

7. Refocus on pleasing God.

In order to eliminate a jealous spirit you must return to your first priority—making certain your life is pleasing to your Creator. *"Let heaven fill your thoughts. Do not think only about things down here on earth"* (Colossians 3:2).

Peter reminds us that the "Chief Shepherd" will appear, so our lives should please Him (1 Peter 5:4 NIV).

When you keep your eyes on the eternal—that which is important to your Maker—the temporal becomes secondary. Suddenly, climbing the ladder of success no longer dominates your time and energy. Yes, you will work diligently to take care of the needs of your family, but your objective rises to a higher plain.

Your directions come from above: *"Lord, don't let me make a mess of things...just tell me what to do and I will do it...turn me away from wanting any other plan than yours"* (Psalm 119:31-37 LB).

Today, thank God for His guidance, trust in His goodness, and delight in His grace.

Thanksgiving is the vaccine for overcoming jealousy —and gratitude is the greatest cure for envy.

CHAPTER **8**

THE "I" INFECTION

Let everyone see that you are
unselfish and considerate in all you do...
— PHILIPPIANS 4:5

A woman lost her handbag in the bustle of Christmas shopping and was delighted when it was found by an honest little boy who returned it to her.

Looking in her purse, she commented, "Hmmm! That's funny. When I lost my purse there was a $20 bill inside. Now there are twenty $1 bills."

The boy quickly replied, "That's right, ma'am. The last time I found a lady's purse, she didn't have any change for a reward!"

Our society is facing an epidemic of selfish living!

Unfortunately, many adults have adopted the "Property Laws of a Toddler" (by an unknown author):

- If I like it, it's mine.
- If it's in my hand, it's mine.

- If I can take it from you, it's mine.
- If I had it a little while ago, it's mine.
- If it's mine, it must not ever appear to be yours in any way.
- If I'm doing or building something, all the pieces are mine.
- If I saw it first, it's mine.
- If it looks just like mine, it's mine.
- If you're playing with something and you put it down, it automatically becomes mine.
- If it's broken, it's yours.

It is one thing to *say* you are an unselfish person, but is this how you act and live? Do you have the courage to give up your rights in order to meet another's needs?

OPEN YOUR HAND

Monkey trappers in some areas of the Far East have a rather clever method of ensnaring the animals.

They take a pumpkin gourd, cut a small hole, then carve out the inside. Next, they take a banana, place it down inside the hollow gourd, stake the gourd to the ground and wait.

Monkeys, being by nature curious creatures, soon descend from the jungle trees. They find the gourd, see the hole, slide their hand inside, discover the banana and grab it—and then pull back.

However, when they try to retract their hand from the gourd, they are frustrated because they can't pull their closed fist back through the small opening.

The only way the monkey's hand can be freed is to release the banana and slide their hand out the same way it went in.

Unwilling to let go of the prize, they hold on tenaciously, then scream and jump—until the trappers come and find them.

What irony! All the monkeys have to do is open their fist and liberty is theirs. By making the wrong choice, they lose their freedom forever.

> **BY MAKING THE WRONG CHOICE, THEY LOSE THEIR FREEDOM FOREVER.**

I've met many individuals who decide to live "close-fisted" lives—thinking only of their own wants and desires. It's a recipe for bondage

THE KEY TO CHANGE

A demonstration of unselfish living is the most powerful tool at our disposal to encourage growth and change in others.

God the Father set the example by giving His most cherished possession—His only Son—as a sacrifice for our sin. *"For God so loved the world, that he gave his only begotten Son, that whosoever believeth in him*

73

should not perish, but have everlasting life" (John 3:16 KJV).

You will never make change happen by placing a "command and control" leader in charge or arguing with an individual until they demonstrate a new behavior.

> PEOPLE ARE TRANSFORMED BY LOVE ACTIONS, NOT LOVE WORDS.

People are transformed by love *actions,* not love words.

After years in ministry and counseling others, I am convinced the way you act and treat others affects your relationship with your Heavenly Father.

Selfishness says, "I am depending on my strength and my power." Prayer says, "I am depending on God."

Look at your own history and ask yourself, "What one person—outside of Christ—has had the greatest influence on my life?"

I'm not a betting man, but if I were, I would wager you would describe your most cherished mentor or role model as "an unselfish person."

THE CURE FOR "I" INFECTION

A man once said, "I'm going away to find myself."

His friend replied, "What you need to do is *lose* yourself!"

Obviously, the man had an "I" problem.

Just because you say "me" more than "we" doesn't mean you must continue living with a selfish attitude. Let me share these remedies:

UNDERSTANDING – Considering another person's needs.

In the context of daily Christian living, the Bible teaches: *"Let everyone see that you are unselfish and considerate in all that you do"* (Philippians 4:5 LB).

Underline three of those words: <u>everyone</u>, <u>unselfish</u> and <u>considerate</u>. These attitudes are to be part of *every* relationship in our lives.

Unselfishness is demonstrated when we ask, "How can I help you?"

It is fundamental to shift our attention from what we desire to what others need.

LISTENING – Hearing what another person says.

The number one barrier to communication is our failure to listen. A conversation is not a solo endeavor, rather it is to establish a connection.

Here are three practical ways to become a competent listener:

1. Be willing to work at it.

We are born with *hearing*, but not with the skill of effective *listening*. It is our human nature to concentrate far more on what *we* say than the words of others.

A conversation is supposed to be circular—I listen, you respond; I respond, you listen. However this "magic circle" breaks down because we are so intent on forming our own thoughts into words we fail to hear what the other person has just said.

Therefore, we need to become an *intentional* listener.

2. Let people say what they want to say—their way.

Perhaps you have noticed that men and women are different when it comes to communication. When a female relates a story, she wants to share the *entire* narrative—from beginning to end, with every juicy detail. Not the male. He gets straight to the point as quickly as possible and wraps it up.

Likewise, listening is affected since the man will literally "turn off" his hearing when he thinks he has heard the gist of a story.

Be sensitive to the speaking style of others by allowing them to tell the narrative *their* way. Also, if you find yourself finishing the sentences of a slow speaker, bite your tongue. Do everything in your power to break the habit.

3. Make eye contact.

Some men pride themselves in the fact they can communicate with their wives while at the same time reading a newspaper, listening to the radio or watching television. However, they are only *half* listening.

People want to *know* we are paying attention—such evidence only comes through eye contact.

Sight has an impact on listening. By looking directly into the eyes, you see *expression* and somehow receive both the spoken and unspoken words.

RESPECT – Honoring another person's value.

Certain people require others to *think* like them and *live* like them as a prerequisite to offering friendship or help. How selfish! It is not only important to understand and listen to the wishes of others, but that you value and esteem their needs.

Here is the biblical position: *"Don't be selfish; don't live to make a good impression on others. Be humble, thinking of others as better than yourself"* (Philippians 2:3).

> RESPECT EVERY PERSON FOR WHO THEY ARE—A UNIQUE AND VALUABLE CHILD OF GOD.

The bottom line? Respect every person for who they are—a unique and valuable child of God.

SACRIFICE – Acting on another person's behalf.

We tell our friends, "I really love you—and would do anything for you." But what happens when you have a golf game scheduled on Saturday afternoon and that's the time when they need some help moving into a new apartment?

Will you pass the "sacrifice" test? Are you simply offering lip service, saying what you think your friend wants to hear—or because it makes *you* feel good?

The Bible tells us, *"Dear children, let us not love with words or tongue but with actions and in truth"* (1 John 3:18 NIV).

It is in the small things of daily living that true sacrifice is demonstrated—not during a major crisis where it is expected.

Today, ask the Lord to completely heal your "I" infection.

> *Open your hand and start giving.*
> *Open your heart and start living.*

CHAPTER 9

FIGHT FAIR

*...be quick to listen, slow to
speak, and slow to get angry.*
— JAMES 1:19

No one has promised you will make it through life without conflict and strife. In fact, the word "fight" occurs over 100 times in the King James Version of the Bible.

Today, when differences of opinion escalate into quarrels and controversy, many choose the option of "flight" rather than "fight." They run from the situation, which only causes their troubles to multiply.

Instead of fleeing, let me recommend a better path—conflict management-developing strategies and attitudes which contribute to peace and harmony.

In the process, you admit there is a personal tug of war; yet, both parties decide on civility rather than hostility. In other words, they choose to "fight fair."

Searching for Answers

Resolving personal conflicts is much like baking a cake; you need the right ingredients. Our recipe includes adding the proper amounts of sympathy, brotherly love, compassion, humility and an extra helping of mercy.

Question #1: What does it mean to be sympathetic?

People often wonder, "Am I the only one thinking this way?" "Am I weird or crazy?" "Does this make sense?"

When you are sympathetic toward others, you are letting them know, "I understand. I value and validate your feelings."

Perhaps you may not see things as they do, or even accept their arguments or ideas, but you are not going to belittle or ridicule their uncertainties. As scripture declares, *"For we must bear the burden of being considerate of the doubts and fears of others..."* (Romans 15:2 LB).

There are two benefits of sympathy: (1) it meets the need of an individual to be understood and (2) it says that a person's feelings are okay.

In the last chapter we discussed the importance of being a good listener. Listening is especially vital as you show someone your really care. When you use your ears more than your mouth, you are communicating, "I am concerned about you."

Question #2: What is brotherly love?

Being committed to a person—regardless of what happens—you demonstrate what it means to *"Be devoted to one another in brotherly love..."* (Romans 12:10 NIV).

Brotherly love shows you are on the same team, part of the same "family" and are complimenting and cooperating with one another. There is no competition.

If you become irritated with a person you truly care about, it is a grave error to suddenly be consumed with only the problem. When that happens, your friend can become your enemy.

Keep your attention on the relationship rather than the disagreement and the tension level will quickly subside.

> KEEP YOUR ATTENTION ON THE RELATIONSHIP RATHER THAN THE DISAGREEMENT AND THE TENSION LEVEL WILL QUICKLY SUBSIDE.

Brotherly love says, "Let's stop attacking each other and start battling the problem together."

Loyalty is a requisite. *"If you love someone you will be loyal to him no matter what the cost"* (1 Corinthians 13:7 LB).

You are saying, "I may differ with you and even become angry at times, but let there be no doubt that I love you and am committed to our relation-ship—regardless!"

Part of being faithful is accepting people as they are.

81

Your love is not dependent on whether or not the person changes their behavior. The Bible tells us, *"Accept one another...just as Christ accepted you..."* (Romans 15:7 NIV).

Question #3: How can compassion be demonstrated?

If sympathy equals understanding someone's feelings, compassion takes it one step further and demonstrates love in action.

It asks the question, "What can I do to help you?"

There are two ways we show compassion:

First: What we say to others and how we say it.

Here is sound advice from the apostle Paul: *"Do not let any unwholesome talk come out of your mouths, but only what is helpful for building others up according to their needs, and that it may benefit those who listen"* (Ephesians 4:29 NIV).

> ARE YOUR
> WORDS TENDER,
> OR ARE
> THEY TOXIC?

Does this admonition characterize your speech? Are your words tender, or are they toxic? Are they meant to build and encourage, or do they injure and destroy?

The right words at the right time can bring healing to a troubled friend.

Second: How we act toward each other.

Compassion is saying with your actions, "How can I

make your life easier?"

You may never need to utter a word—just your countenance and a gentle hug can communicate everything needed. As the Bible counsels, *"...clothe yourselves with compassion"* (Colossians 3:12 NIV).

Question #4: What is the test of humility?

John Brodie, former multi-million dollar quarterback for the San Francisco 49ers, was once asked, "Why do you, the quarterback, hold the football for the extra point kick after a touchdown?"

"Well," he said, "if I didn't it would fall over!"

Brodie had a humble spirit, he wasn't "too good" for *any* assignment.

What is humility? It is:

- Being honest about my weaknesses.
- Not assuming I know everything you are talking about.
- Being willing to acknowledge my errors.

King Solomon wrote: *"Anyone who refuses to admit his mistakes can never be successful. But if he confesses and forsakes them, he gets another chance"* (Proverbs 28:13 LB).

Remember, true love is not proud or arrogant.

Question #5: How do I extend mercy?

According to history, a mother visited Napoleon to plead for her condemned son's life. The great warrior and Emperor of France told her the young man had committed the same serious offence *twice*—and justice warranted the death penalty.

"Sir," the mother pleaded, "I am not asking for justice, I am asking for mercy."

"He doesn't deserve it," Napoleon shot back.

"No, he doesn't," said the mother, "but then if he did it would not be mercy."

Napoleon turned and stated, "I grant mercy."

The story illustrates one of my favorite definitions of mercy: giving more kindness than justice demands.

When things go wrong in our personal relationships, we have a choice: retaliation or reconciliation. The apostle Peter tells us, *"Don't repay evil for evil. Don't retaliate when people say unkind things about you. Instead, pay them back with a blessing. That is what God wants you to do, and he will bless you for it"* (1 Peter 3:9).

Our decision should be easy. Since we have been pardoned by God far more than we can ever pardon anyone on earth, we need to dispense mass doses of mercy. *"Remember, the Lord forgave you, so you must forgive others"* (Colossians 3:13).

Grow Up Without Growing Old

Mastering the art of treating others with sympathy, brotherly love, compassion, humility and mercy is a sure sign of maturity.

How can you know if you have reached this level or not? It is when your concern for others is greater than your concern for yourself.

It's not your age, but your *actions*, which really count.

The conflicts in our relationships will become a distant memory when we practice friendliness, fairness and forgiveness.

CHAPTER 10

CAN'T GET NO SATISFACTION!

*You will never be satisfied if you long
to be rich. You will never get all you want.*
— ECCLESIASTES 5:10 TEV

The Milton Bradley company has a game called "Mall Madness." The objective is "Will you be the first to lose all your money?"

The description says: You are let loose in a shopping mall with $200. Go to it and spend it all. Empty your pockets first and you win the game. When you have spent every cent, your marker moves triumphantly into the middle space entitled "Broke" — and you are the winner.

In a recent survey of female teenagers, 93% said their number one pastime was shopping. It beat out dating as their favorite activity.

I laughed when I heard one man comment, "If my wife doesn't go to the mall three times a week, I send her a get well card!"

THE DESIRE TO ACQUIRE

Why is it so difficult for most people to be content with what they have? They seem to have an insatiable urge to hoard more and more—the desire to acquire.

This impulse doesn't have to be a negative. For example, God gave squirrels a natural instinct to store up acorns so they would be fed in the winter. He gave birds the desire to gather straw so they will have nests to live in.

The problem occurs when our urges become uncontrollable—mistaking our need for our greed!

THE FOUR DANGERS OF DISCONTENTMENT

It seems we are never satisfied.

I recall the story of a man whose girlfriend kept refusing to marry him. "I don't understand," he asked her, "is there someone else?

With a sigh, she answered, "There has to be!"

This attitude is reflected almost everywhere we turn—"Surely there is something better!"

Sadly, discontentment is accompanied by hidden dangers:

One: The danger of fatigue.

In our push to have more, we often find ourselves

exhausted. We take second and third jobs in order to buy more things for the family we say we love. However, because of this urge to acquire we become burned out and fatigued.

Listen to God's warning: *"Do not wear yourself out to be rich; have the wisdom to show restraint"* (Proverbs 23:4 NIV).

Two: The danger of debt.

A wife complained to her husband, "It's not that I spend too much, it's that you deposit too little!"

A recent report stated the average American puts $1300 on credit for every $1000 he or she makes. That's called deficit spending—and the only institution supposed to get away with deficit spending is the federal government!

Debt is the result of uncontrollable desire. *"The more money you have, the more money you spend..."* (Ecclesiastes 5:11 LB).

In the words of an astute observer, "If the grass is greener on the other side of the fence, you can bet the water bill is higher, too!"

Make sure your self-control includes debt control!

Three: The danger of worry.

When your focus is on material possessions (money included), you constantly worry about your "stuff":

- How am I going to keep it?

- How am I going to save it?
- How am I going to invest it?
- How am I going to insure it?
- How am I going to protect it?

According to scripture, insomnia increases with income. *"People who work hard sleep well, whether they eat little or much. But the rich are always worrying and seldom get a good night's sleep"* (Ecclesiastes 5:12).

Four: The danger of dissatisfaction.

Your possessions may produce contentment for a while; however, the thrill doesn't last. *"It is foolish to think that wealth brings happiness"* (Ecclesiastes 5:10 LB).

Physical objects never satisfy for long. You become bored with your car, your house and your furniture. Why? Because "things" don't change; you change!

—— ❧ ——
PHYSICAL OBJECTS NEVER SATISFY FOR LONG.

"Planned obsolescence" is what greases the rails of the fashion and advertising industry. If styles don't become outdated, sales plummet.

We are willing accomplices. And if we cannot purchase the new model, we redecorate, repair or rearrange, trying to be happy once more.

How easily we fall prey to the peril of dissatisfaction—the menace of wanting "more."

TRAPPED BY DESIRES

Failure to deal with discontentment leads you to eventually think you are what you *do*—or you are what you *possess*. Your life becomes a vicious circle of being all things to all people, striving to impress and spending every waking moment chasing another dollar.

What is the result? You set unrealistic goals and lose a sense of personal satisfaction by never reaching your objective. Even worse, when you compare yourself with those who have reached their more attainable objectives, you bury your head in your hands and say, "I'm a big loser!" The loss of self-esteem can't be measured.

Here are the facts: people *"...who long to be rich fall into temptation and are trapped by many foolish and harmful desires that plunge them into ruin and destruction"* (1 Timothy 6:9).

THE SECRET!

Contentment doesn't come naturally. It is something we learn. The apostle Paul said, *"I have learned the secret of being content in any and every situation..."* (Philippians 4:12).

Over the years I've learned three very important lessons from some very successful people in my life. Especially my dear friend Keith Rochester (now with God in heaven) who demonstrated how to:

Admire without having to acquire.

Don't be uptight over the success of your neighbor.

Work on being able to admire the new car of a friend or the new furnishings of a neighbor's home without being bitter over the fact you can't purchase similar items.

I heard about a man who was visiting the lavish home of a life-long friend who proudly pointed out, "This furniture goes all the way back to Louis the 8th."

"Wow! smiled the guest, "Our furniture goes back to Sears on the 15th—if we fail to make our payment."

Overcome "when and then" thinking.

Millions are caught up in the false premise of "When I get this, then I will be content." They think, "I'll be happy...":

- When I buy a new car.
- When I get married.
- When I move into a new home.
- When I get a promotion.
- When I have children.

_____ ✷ _____
STOP SEARCHING FOR EXTERNALS TO MEASURE YOUR SUCCESS.

Stop searching for externals to measure your success. Thank the Lord for giving you breath and life—anything else is a pure bonus from your Heavenly Father. Scripture tells us, *"...when God gives any man wealth and possessions, and enables him to enjoy them, to accept his lot and be happy in his work—this is a gift of God"* (Ecclesiastes 5:19 NIV).

Become a generous giver.

Over the years I've been blessed—and impressed by some extremely generous people. I've leaned from them how generosity is one way to keep life on track.

Paul gives this advice to young Timothy: *"Tell those who are rich not to be proud and not to trust in their money, which will soon be gone...Tell them to use their money to do well* [and] *give happily to those in need, always being ready to share with others whatever God has given them. By doing this they will be storing up real treasure for themselves in heaven—it is the only safe investment for eternity!"* (1 Timothy 6:17-19).

You may read the first words of this passage and think, "This isn't about me. I'm not rich!"

The truth is if you are alive in America, regardless of your net worth, compared to the rest of the world you are in the top three percent.

Even if your bank balance is a big fat "zero," you live in a land of opportunity and freedom where the sky is the limit. Plus, as a child of God, you have an inner peace which cannot be measured with gold or silver. Even more, you are an heir to your Father's Kingdom!

The challenge in Paul's writing is for us to be generous with what we *do* have, since it is an eternal investment.

WEALTH VS. MATERIALISM

Is it possible to be wealthy without being materialistic? It all depends on your attitude.

I've met poor people who are greedy and rich people who are greedy. The opposite is also true. The impoverished can be just as content as those with unlimited finances.

If you want to avoid the trap of materialism, let me suggest these four precautions:

First: Don't become proud or your possessions.

The man who constantly brags of what money can buy will soon be left with what's in his wallet. His friends will abandon him. Why? Because we can only tolerate a bragger in small doses.

Second: Don't put your trust in money.

If you think your security rests in your bank account, read the stories of those who experienced the Great Depression. Entire life savings were wiped out in a single day!

Third: Use your money for the right reasons.

Wasteful, selfish spending is an affront to God. He has blessed you with abundance for a purpose—to build God's Kingdom, to provide for your family and to help those less fortunate than yourself.

Fourth: Give cheerfully.

The root of materialism is "Get! Get! Get!" The polar opposite is "Give! Give! Give!" So every time you are generous, you are helping to defeat the grip of "possessions" on your life. Remember, *"More blessings come from giving than from receiving"* (Acts 20:35 CEV).

What a profound difference it makes when this verse becomes a lifestyle rather than a phrase.

INVISIBLE VALUES

As a parent, it melts your heart when the time finally arrives that your children are just as excited about seeing you open the Christmas presents they have given as the ones they have received.

Just imagine how the Lord must feel when He looks down and sees His children sharing—having more joy in giving than getting.

> WHEN GIVING COMES FROM THE HEART, THERE IS AN INVISIBLE VALUE WHICH CAN'T BE MEASURED.

When giving comes from the heart, there is an invisible value which can't be measured. Hence, we must, *"...fix our attention not on things that are seen, but on things that are unseen"* (2 Corinthians 4:18 TEV).

ULTIMATE SATISFACTION

The desire for what is "bigger and better" warps your

perspective and clouds your vision of God. Jesus spoke of this truth when He gave us the parable of a wealthy farmer.

One particular year the man had a bumper crop—so much so he didn't have room to store the overflow.

He thought, *"I know! I'll tear down my barns and build bigger ones. Then I'll have room enough to store everything. And I'll sit back and say to myself, My friend, you have enough stored away for years to come. Now take it easy! Eat, drink, and be merry!"* (Luke 12:18-19).

It never occurred to the wealthy farmer to share what he had—or even to tithe on his bounty.

God said to him, *"'You fool! You will die this very night. Then who will get it all?' Yes, a person is a fool to store up earthly wealth but not have a rich relationship with God"* (v.20).

What we accumulate may be for sixty or seventy years, and then it's gone. But remember the words of Jesus, *"Real life is not measured by how much we own"* (Luke 12:15).

Everything we possess is fleeting and will rust, decay and fall apart. The only things which truly last are invisible—your love, your values, your family and your relationship with God.

These are you source of ultimate satisfaction.

Why run away from yourself when contentment is only a prayer away?

CHAPTER 11

HURTING ON
THE INSIDE

*Put your heart right, reach out to God...then
face the world again, firm and courageous. Then all
your troubles will fade from your memory, like floods
that are past and remembered no more.*

– JOB 11:13-16 TEV

We are about to find solutions for one of the most deep-seated issues of life.

I remember hearing Rick Warren speak on the theme life's invisible pain and he asked his audience to take this health survey:

- Have you ever required stitches?
- Have you ever been stabbed?
- Have you ever been shot?
- Have you ever been wounded in a war?

- Have you ever needed surgery?

Regardless of your answers, there is a common denominator among all of these questions. They all involve open, public wounds.

However, as I have personally discovered, the most severe agony you will ever experience comes from what you cannot see—the hidden hurts caused by deep, distressing memories. You may have kept them a secret; yet, they continue to resurface, causing repeated anguish.

These are the invisible scars of ridicule, rejection, abandonment or unfaithfulness. In fact, I have yet to counsel with an individual who did not have some kind of hidden wound.

"WHAT SHOULD I DO?"

Without exception, the damage to our thoughts and emotions can be directly traced to the actions of people. We were not born with these injuries, they were inflicted upon us—from bullies on the school playground to the trauma of abuse by a family member.

Rather than relive the problems, which we know are real, let me offer solutions. Certainly, there is a place for professional Christian counseling; but I believe you can apply these scripture-based answers regardless of what has caused your pain.

Forgive the offender.

Angry, you might say, "I don't want to forgive. They

don't deserve it!" Even if your feelings are justified, forgiveness is rarely deserved—still, it is a necessary requirement for restoration.

As you read the story of the crucifixion, you realize Jesus endured physical wounds. His flesh was torn in several places. There were stripes on His back, nail prints in His hands and feet, and a crown of thorns pierced His brow. As Peter writes, *"So then, since Christ suffered physical pain, you must arm yourselves with the same attitude he had"* (1 Peter 4:1).

The visual image of His suffering, as was so compellingly demonstrated in *The Passion of the Christ*, can cause us to forget Christ also experienced some of life's most serious hidden wounds—betrayal, hatred and prejudice.

How did Jesus respond? He simply looked up to heaven and said, *"Father, forgive them, for they do not know what they are doing"* (Luke 23:34).

According to scripture, He could have declared "Enough is enough" and called ten thousand angels to save Him. Instead, Jesus chose to offer pardon.

IF YOU ARE EVER GOING TO RISE ABOVE YOUR INNER PAIN, YOU MUST FORGIVE THE OFFENDER.

If you are ever going to rise above your inner pain, you must forgive the offender. Why? There are two reasons: first, because God has so mercifully forgiven you. Second, you will need forgiveness in the future, so

99

never burn the bridge that you may one day need to cross.

Until you release the distress, it will continue to fester and grow. The Bible tells us: *"Watch out that no bitterness takes root among you, for as it springs up it causes deep trouble, hurting many in their spiritual lives"* (Hebrews 12:15 LB)

————— ✸ —————
BY FANNING THE FLAMES OF UNFORGIVENESS YOU ARE CONTINUALLY BURNED BY THE COALS.

The result of an unforgiving spirit is resentment— which always brings more harm to you than to the offender. As you constantly replay the incident of the past in your memory bank, the person who has hurt you has likely forgotten all about it and gone on with his life. However, by fanning the flames of unforgiveness you are continually burned by the coals. As a result, *"You are only hurting yourself with your anger!"* (Job 18:4 TEV).

Focus on the Healer, not the hurt.

Divert your attention from your problem to the Problem Solver. This requires a mental shift, yet it is a must.

I am not suggesting you *ignore* your past. You couldn't if you tried. As a matter of fact, it is all right to express your sorrow over yesterday. Jesus tells us, *"Blessed are those who mourn, for they will be comforted"* (Matthew 5:4).

A well known minister reminded his congregation

about the difference between *mourning* and *moaning!"*

I remember him saying:

- Mourning says, "I am sad this happened to me."
- Moaning says, "I'll never get over it. This will plague me for the rest of my life."
- Mourning says, "I am hurt, but I'll be okay."
- Moaning says, "Let me have my pity party!"

The point is, if you remain stuck in the past you can't get on with the present—or the future.

Allow the Great Physician to bring a positive purpose out of your pain. *"From now on, live the rest of your earthly lives controlled by God's will, not by human desires"* (1 Peter 4:2 TEV).

Learn to trust God—allow Him to settle the score.

Instead of plotting your revenge, let the Lord balance the books, just as Jesus did at the cross. In the midst of His suffering, *"...he did not threaten to get even. He left his case in the hands of God, who always judges fairly"* (1 Peter 2:23 LB).

Many of us forget that our Heavenly Father sees every trial we go through. As David told the Lord, *"You [God] know how troubled I am; You have kept a record of my tears"* (Psalm 56:8 TEV).

God even sees those concealed tears you couldn't

shed because of the deep inner pain. Your suffering, large or small, matters to the Lord.

Subconsciously we hold onto our hurts because we believe, "Somebody has to remember how bad this was." We are afraid if we forget the matter, the person who harmed us will escape with no punishment.

Since God keeps an account, retribution should not be a concern. By faith, let go and trust your Father to deal fairly with the situation. Allow Him to settle the score.

Face the world again.

Transformation begins by asking the Lord to cleanse your heart and making a decision to leave the rest to history. Now you are ready to *"face the world again, firm and courageous..."* (Job 11:15 TEV)—strong and free of fear.

The Lord is encouraging you to stop living in denial. Saying, "It doesn't hurt," won't alter the facts.

Instead of masking your feelings or trying to cover them up, ask God to help you face reality and move forward.

Turn your eyes to the future.

The turning point of forgetting is to refocus—shifting gears from the past to the present, and beyond.

However, in the depths of a crisis, I've heard people cry, "I just can't face the future!"

At this point total trust in the Almighty becomes your strength. Pour out your heart to Him. Perhaps you will admit, "Lord, I am hurt. I'm depressed and afraid. I blame this individual for what has been done to me."

Through honesty and releasing your feelings to God, you open up those hidden wounds and clear the way for the Lord to pour in His healing balm.

Sadly, instead of taking this step, many look for a quick fix and turn to alcohol or, if the stress becomes unbearable, will swallow a few "happy" pills. Others, to help ease the loneliness, settle for a one night stand. These choices just compound the problem.

> THE WORLD CAN OFFER ONLY TEMPORARY PAIN KILLERS, AND WHEN THE PARTY IS OVER, THE HURT RETURNS.

The world can offer only temporary pain killers, and when the party is over, the hurt returns.

Rest in this assurance: *"The Lord hears his people when they call to him for help. He rescues them from all their troubles. The Lord is close to the brokenhearted; he rescues those who are crushed in spirit"* (Psalm 34:17-18)

When you turn your eyes toward the future, God will not only show you a bright tomorrow, He will allow your memories of the past to dim and fade.

Find your place with others.

You will never be completely whole until you are

able to share your life with caring people. Accept help and encouragement by way of support groups, friends and others.

God does not intend for us to solve our problems by ourselves. After the Creator formed Adam, He said, *"It is not good for the man to be alone. I will make a companion who will help him"* (Genesis 2:18).

There is enormous healing power released through those who love us—starting with the Lord Himself.

We are told to *"...love each other deeply, because love covers over a multitude of sins. Offer hospitality to one another..."* (1 Peter 4:8-9 NIV).

Why do you require supportive relationships? *"Two people can accomplish more than twice as much as one; they get a better return for their labor. If one person falls, the other can reach out and help. But people who are alone when they fall are in real trouble"* (Ecclesiastes 4:9-10).

We need each other!

DON'T HESITATE

If you are serious about getting your life back on track, don't pretend the trauma never happened. The Lord knows what you have endured and with compassion is waiting at this moment for you to have an open, honest talk with Him.

That divine conversation may lead you to take some

uncomfortable steps—including reaching out to forgive the one who has caused you so much heartache and unhappiness.

Don't hesitate or be afraid. I believe it will be one of the most liberating moments of your life.

No matter how deep the wounds may be, you have a loving God who will heal your hurts and set you free.

CHAPTER 12

TRIUMPHANTLY MEET TEMPTATION

*But remember that the temptations that
come into your life are no different from
what others experience. And God is faithful.
He will keep the temptation from becoming so
strong that you can't stand up against it. When
you are tempted, he will show you a way
out so that you will not give in to it.*
— 1 CORINTHIANS 10:13

He was behind bars, serving time for crimes he had committed. Yet he was a Christian and asked if the visiting minister could send him some books which were not available in the prison library.

The clergyman gladly responded to the request and, in doing so, discovered some interesting facts about this young man.

He learned he was a student of an outstanding theological seminary and graduated with great promise and a strong vision. He pastored two different churches—both with thriving, growing congregations.

The young man was a dedicated student of the Bible, and many who had heard him preach spoke of how they could sense the power and the presence of God in his life.

Now he was a prisoner in a state penal institution.

How did this happen? In one dark hour of temptation, he fell into sin. He ruined his reputation, destroyed his ministry and left an ugly stain on the testimony of Christ in his community.

KNOWING OUR FOE

Even the strongest of God's children falter and make mistakes. It is not being tempted which is an undercurrent of life; rather, it is *falling* into temptation which can, and will, catch up with you.

God expects us to triumphantly face enticement; however, we must first understand the nature of what we are up against.

Temptation comes in disguise.

I remember the story of a wife who had an alcoholic husband. After she had used every possible tactic to stop her spouse from drinking, the woman decided to resort to fear.

One night she dressed up in a "devil" costume—including a long red tail, horns and a pitchfork.

The woman waited patiently in the dark until her inebriated husband came around the corner of the kitchen. She jumped out and screamed, "I'm the devil. And if you don't stop drinking I'm going to get you!"

Before she could get another word out of her mouth, her husband put out his hand and said, "Glad to meet you. I married your sister!"

In real life, though, our adversary does not make his appearance in his traditional "garb."

Don't expect temptation to appear in the form of a coiled snake, with the wail of a siren or the waving of a red flag, shouting, "Here I am. Watch out for me!"

> SATAN ARRIVES SILENTLY AND INCOGNITO— ALMOST LIKE A COMFORTABLE COMPANION.

Instead, Satan arrives silently and incognito—almost like a comfortable companion. He masquerades his persona, and also his purpose.

Jesus said the devil *"...was a murderer from the beginning and has always hated the truth. There is no truth in him. When he lies, it is consistent with his character; for he is a liar and the father of lies"* (John 8:44).

Temptation attacks divine principles.

We see the influence of a godless media in novels where the author manipulates the plot so the characters live in deep disobedience to God, yet at the end, everything turns out rosy. And, in movies heroes rebel against moral laws, then go on to live happily ever after.

_____ ✞ _____

LITTLE BY LITTLE, THE DEVIL AND HIS MINIONS UNDERMINE SPIRITUAL PRINCIPLES.

Little by little, the devil and his minions undermine spiritual principles. Their objective is to have you doubt the seriousness of God's judgment on sin and disobedience.

Temptation attacks God's character.

Starting with Adam and Eve, our evil foe waged an attack on the authority and attributes of the Creator.

In the Garden of Eden, God gave the first couple total freedom to enjoy the fruit of any plant except one. He told them, "If you eat from the Tree of the Knowledge of Good and Evil you will die."

The serpent slithered up to Eve and explained, "Surely God didn't mean that. You won't really die!" And he hissed, _"God knows that your eyes will be opened when you eat it. You will become just like God, knowing everything, both good and evil"_ (Genesis 3:5).

For thousands of years, Satan has repeated his devious strategy—slandering God's name and character.

Consequently, it is vital to know how the devil operates.

WHAT ARE THE CONSEQUENCES?

The next time temptation crosses you path, consider these questions:

What effect will this have on me?

As you come face to face with any "forbidden fruit," pause, take a few steps back and ask yourself, "What will be the ultimate outcome of my decision? What will it do to my body, my mind, my reputation, my spiritual life?"

What will this lead to?

There is no such thing as enjoying the pleasure of a sin and not suffering the consequences and penalties. Perhaps you have a friend who made a moral mistake. Was there a price to be paid? Were family members or children hurt?

Every time you succumb to one of the devil's false promises you open another door which leads even deeper into his trap. Is it really worth the risk?

What effect will this have on God's Kingdom?

It's rather egotistical to think your actions will only impact you! Your good name—and the name of your family are at stake. If you call yourself a child of God, you also have an obligation to your Heavenly Father. So, *"whatever you do or say, let it be as a representative of the Lord Jesus..."* (Colossians 3:17).

The reason for our existence as a believer is to serve Christ and bring honor and glory to His name.

CAN YOU PASS THE TEST?

I have been asked, "Pastor, how can I really know the difference between a harmless act and yielding to a temptation?"

It was a wise and discerning mother who asked her children to consider these "tests" when temptation comes:

1. The test of secrecy.

A husband and wife were discussing the subject of who could best keep a secret, male or female?

The husband said, "A woman's idea of keeping a secret is not telling who told it!"

His wife replied, "That's not true. A woman can keep a secret as good as any man. It just takes more of us to do it!"

When you are at a point of indecision, ask yourself, "Are there those I'd be ashamed to tell of my behavior?" How about your parents? Would they be proud of your actions?

If your behavior won't pass the "secrecy" test, consider it a red flag!

2. The test of universality.

Would it be okay for *everyone* to do exactly what you are about to do? What kind of family, community or world would we live in if every person behaved this same way?

3. The test of prayer.

Do you feel comfortable asking the Lord to bless you in this activity? Can you sincerely answer the question, "Is this what Jesus would do?"

In the words of the English clergyman Studdert Kennedy, "Prayer is not an easy way of getting what we want, but the only way of becoming what God wants us to be."

IF YOU FEEL HESITANT TO TAKE IT TO THE LORD IN PRAYER, YOU'D BETTER RECONSIDER AND BACK AWAY FROM THE BEHAVIOR.

If you feel hesitant to take it to the Lord in prayer, you'd better reconsider and back away from the behavior.

"A WAY OUT"

When the allures of this world seem overpowering, allow the Lord to do what He does best—to protect you with His mighty hand.

Remember, *"Since he himself has gone through suffering and temptation, he is able to help us when we are being tempted"* (Hebrews 2:18). Remember, *"...he will show you a way out so that you will not give in to it"* (1 Corinthians 10:13).

What a promise!

**The seduction of this world may try
to ensnare me, but with God's help I will
meet temptation triumphantly.**

CHAPTER 13

THE MOST ELUSIVE SEARCH OF ALL

Though a man lives a thousand years twice over but doesn't find contentment—what's the use?
– ECCLESIASTES 6:6 LB

Freddie Mercury, the lead singer of Queen, was the first major rock star to die of AIDS. The benefit concert to his memory packed Wembley Stadium in London—and had an estimated television audience of one billion around the world.

At the height of his career, Freddie sang these lyrics: "What is there left for me to do in this life? Did I achieve what I had set in my sights; am I a happy man or is this sinking sand? Was it all worth it?"

SOLOMON'S QUEST

Centuries ago, a man named Solomon was at the top

of the ladder, the pinnacle of success. He was the undisputed leader of the most influential nation at the time, yet he admitted, "Everything is meaningless."

This wise man concluded, *"Though a man lives a thousand years twice over, but doesn't find contentment—well, what's the use?"* (Ecclesiastes 6:6 LB).

Solomon began a search of trying to find the true meaning of life. One particular question for which he sought the answer was, "How can I find happiness?" It is still a universal quest.

THE MORE HE LEARNED, THE MORE HE REALIZED HE DIDN'T KNOW!

He was in a unique situation to pursue this matter since he had both the intellect and the money to carry out his research. Plus, as king, he had plenty of time.

The biblical account is clear; Solomon considered five areas as he pursued happiness:

1. Education.

King Solomon tried to find happiness through academic pursuits, but the more he learned the more he realized how much he didn't know!

He admitted, *"...I am better educated than any of the kings before me... [but] the more my wisdom, the more my grief..."* (Ecclesiastes 1:16-18 LB).

Education increased his questions but rendered no ultimate satisfaction.

2. Pleasure.

Next, he tried to entertain himself—believing a good laugh and a glass of wine was all he needed.

As he explained, *"I said to myself, 'Come now, let's give pleasure a try. Let's look for the "good things" in life.' But I found that this, too, was meaningless. 'It is silly to be laughing all the time,' I said. 'What good does it do to seek only pleasure?' After much thought, I decided to cheer myself with wine. While still seeking wisdom, I clutched at foolishness. In this way, I hoped to experience the only happiness most people find during their brief life in this world"* (Ecclesiastes 2:1-3).

Solomon became the "party animal" of his day, intent on enjoying all the fun he could. If you read the story further, you'll find he bought a harem and tried to satisfy himself through sexual escapades.

Nothing worked—not even the wine, the oldest mood-enhancing drug in the world. He discovered pleasure always promises more than it can deliver.

3. Diligent work.

In his search, Solomon decided to immerse himself in work. He wrote, *"I also tried to find meaning by building huge homes for myself and by planting beautiful vineyards. I made gardens and parks, filling them with all kinds of fruit trees"* (Ecclesiastes 2:4-5).

A biographer of president Lyndon B. Johnson recorded that toward the end of his days, Johnson asked,

"Can you make something meaningful of my life?"

4. Wealth

"I will try money," the king said. "Surely it will satisfy."

He recalled, *"I bought slaves, both men and women, and others were born into my household. I also owned great herds and flocks, more than any of the kings who lived in Jerusalem before me. I collected great sums of silver and gold, the treasure of many kings and provinces. I hired wonderful singers, both men and women, and had many beautiful concubines. I had everything a man could desire!"* (Ecclesiastes 2:7-8).

When you account for inflation, Solomon was the richest man who ever lived. Still, there was no satisfaction.

5. Achievement

If personal accomplishments and the praise of men could produce contentment, Solomon would have been blissfully happy. Yet, there remained a deep, hollow place inside.

Here's how he described his feelings: *"I became greater than any of the kings who ruled in Jerusalem before me. And with it all, I remained clear-eyed so that I could evaluate all these things. Anything I wanted, I took. I did not restrain myself from any joy...But as I looked at everything I had worked so hard to accomplish, it was all so meaningless...There was nothing really worthwhile anywhere"* (vv. 9-11).

What was the bottom line result of Solomon's search? He said, *"So I hated life, because the work that is done under the sun was grievous to me. All of it is meaningless, a chasing after the wind"* (Ecclesiastes 2:17).

His earthly pursuits were elusive.

JESUS' EIGHT KEYS TO HAPPINESS

Where do you turn when, like Solomon of old, you have tried everything under the sun to attain peace and contentment? Let me recommend living by the "Beatitutes"—a word which is defined as "supreme well being."

These are the secrets of life which Jesus taught at the beginning of the Sermon on the Mount. Some have called them the "Be-Attitudes" since this is how the Lord desires us to *be*.

> *WHERE DO YOU TURN WHEN, LIKE SOLOMON OF OLD, YOU HAVE TRIED EVERYTHING UNDER THE SUN TO FIND PEACE AND CONTENTMENT?*

1. Get to know God.

"How happy are those who know their need is for God" (Matthew 5:3 PT).

The first step to satisfaction is to recognize that your

real hunger—the ache in your heart—is for your Creator.

God not only made you with a physical body and an intellect, you are also a spiritual being. Until you come to the place where you freely admit your need is for the Almighty, you will never, *ever* be happy.

Jesus did not say, "How happy are those who know their need is for money—or fame, or success." Our need is for God.

When the Lord is not at the very core of your life, you are discontented, regardless of what you may have chosen to surround yourself with.

As Saint Augustine expressed, "Thou has made us for Thyself, O Lord; and our hearts are restless until they rest in Thee."

2. Trust the Father in disappointing times.

"Happy are those who mourn; God will comfort them!" (Matthew 5:4 GN).

Jesus is referring to life being a combination of pleasure and pain. It is not all fun and games, but often filled with heartaches.

The person who thinks, "I have to live problem-free in order to be happy," will likely be miserable most of his days.

You have to learn to be content in the *valley* of the shadow—even if you're unemployed or lying in a hospital bed. Say with the psalmist, *"Your promise revives me; it comforts me in all my troubles"* (Psalm 119:50).

3. Expect the Almighty to meet your needs.

"Happy are those who claim nothing, for the whole earth belongs to them!" (Matthew 5:4 GN).

Instead of frantically trying to grab all you can and saying, "This is mine," just relax. As a child of God, everything on this planet is yours!

Don't expect your husband, wife, boyfriend, boss—or even the government—to meet your needs. You already possess everything required.

Since the treasures of this world are yours, God expects you to be a giver, not a taker. It's one more key to contentment.

> SINCE THE TREASURES OF THIS WORLD ARE YOURS, GOD EXPECTS YOU TO BE A GIVER, NOT A TAKER.

In Solomon's search for happiness, he uses the terms *me, my* or *mine* 35 times. He talks about "My pleasure. My happiness. My success." Since he was so self-absorbed it's no wonder he was dissatisfied.

The "me-only" person who achieves all his desires is still left empty because he has to live with himself!

When you form a partnership with God, He will meet your needs—and much more.

4. Follow God's instructions.

"Happy are those whose greatest desire is to do what God requires; God will satisfy them fully" (Matthew 5:6 GN).

Life is not to endure, but to enjoy. It may come as a surprise to some when they learn the Lord actually wants us to have fun on our spiritual journey. Young Timothy is reminded, *"God...richly give us all we need for our enjoyment"* (1 Timothy 6:17).

The Lord created certain principles for us to follow. Obeying them results in enormous benefits, but ignoring them leads to destruction; they are given for a purpose—to give us joy on our journey and keep us headed in the right direction.

> ___ ❧ ___
> THE REASON GOD HAS LAID DOWN SPECIFIC GUIDELINES IS TO KEEP YOUR LIFE RUNNING SMOOTHLY.

It is much like a train running down the tracks. The train complains, "I hate these rails. I can only go where they lead me. I think I will jump off the tracks and go my own way." When he does he crashes and burns.

The reason God has laid down specific guidelines is to keep your life running smoothly.

For total inner peace, follow God's will *completely.*

5. Cultivate a merciful heart.

"Happy are the kind and merciful, for they will be

122

shown mercy" (Matthew 5:7 GN).

Two of the great enemies of happiness are bitterness and resentment.

Sure you're going to be upset when others treat you unfairly. Whether it is unintentional or on purpose isn't the issue. The question is how will you respond?

If you choose to be filled with rancor and resentment—holding onto grudges against those who offend—you are only hurting yourself.

The message of Jesus is, for your own sake, cultivate a merciful, forgiving heart.

Do whatever it takes to exchange your bitterness for mercy.

6. Maintain a clear conscience.

"Happy are the pure in heart; they will see God" (Matthew 5:8 GN).

Guilt is one more thief of your joy.

If you know your behavior is not pleasing in God's sight, yet you plow ahead anyway, the remorse and self-reproach will suffocate any happiness.

Accordingly, the most contented people on earth are those who live with integrity.

Jesus died on the cross so we could be guilt-free. Allow Him to wipe the slate clean and you will know the peace of having a clear conscience.

7. Build healthy relationships.

"Happy are the peacemakers" (Matthew 5:9 GN).

The annals of history are filled with the accounts of people who built great careers but lost their family. Even when faced with the reality of divorce, they chose their business pursuits rather than becoming a peacemaker at home and reconciling relationships.

> **WHAT HAVE YOU GAINED IF YOU RISE TO THE TOP, YET HAVE NO ONE WITH WHOM TO SHARE YOUR ACCOMPLISHMENTS?**

It doesn't matter how much is in your bank account or the number of plaques adorning your walls. What have you gained if you rise to the top, yet have no one with whom to share your accomplishments?

Perhaps you have been on the fast track so long you haven't stopped long enough to build healthy friendships. It will be one of the great regrets of your life.

Here is what the Lord tells us: *"Change your ways. Encourage each other. Live in harmony and peace. Then the God of love and peace will be with you"* (2 Corinthians 13:11).

8. Live with an eternal perspective.

"Happy are those who are persecuted because they are good...a tremendous reward awaits you in heaven" (Matthew 5:9-10 GN).

In other words, don't just look at the here and now.

Jesus does not say, "Happy are those who are persecuted because they are religious fanatics and irritate people around them." No, He says if you do "good" and are harassed and oppressed, you still have something to rejoice about. There's a better day coming!

I pray you will use these keys offered by the Lord. When you do, your search for happiness will no longer elude you.

Doing what is convenient is much easier than doing what is right—yet it makes the difference between a temporary or an eternal reward.

CHAPTER 14

M-PATIENT

Better a patient man than a warrior, a man
who controls his temper than one who takes a city.
– PROVERBS 16:32 NIV

Let me tell you the story of a young man named Daniel "Rudy" Ruettiger.

As a high school football player, his dream was to make it to college and play for the Notre Dame Fighting Irish. However, his father and brother, not wanting him to be disappointed, told him, "Don't get your hopes up. It will never happen."

You see, Rudy was only 5'6" and weighed 165 pounds. Plus, his grades weren't much to brag about, so he joined the Navy. But at the age of 23, he enrolled at a junior college in South Bend, Indiana, and supported himself working as a groundskeeper at Notre Dame's Knute Rockne Stadium.

On three separate occasions he tried to transfer to

Notre Dame, but was rejected each time. Undeterred, on the fourth try he succeeded.

Rudy's football dream was still alive and because of his tenacity he won a non-scholarship spot on the practice team. Though the scrimmages were rough and he was often injured, his spirit wasn't dampened. Still, he was not allowed to suit up for the actual games.

His commitment earned him the respect of his teammates and coaches. Then, on November 8, 1975, for the final home game of his senior year, coach Dan Devine allowed Rudy to suit up.

During the last moments of the game with Georgia Tech, the fans in the stand and the players on the sidelines suddenly began chanting, "Rudy! Rudy! Rudy!"

With only 27 seconds remaining on the clock, the coach put him in. To everyone's amazement, he sacked the quarterback—and the stadium went wild.

To this day, Rudy is still the only player in Notre Dame's history to be carried off the field on his teammates' shoulders.

Why is Rudy Ruettiger still a legend to Fighting Irish fans? It is because of his patience and determination.

POISE, COMPOSURE AND CALM

Many find patience a difficult virtue. Consider our vocabulary.

We:

- Leap out of bed.
- Bolt off to work.
- Run through our schedule.
- Scramble to close the deal.
- Wolf down our sandwich.
- Get crackin' on a final project.
- Race home in rush hour traffic.
- Dart in the front door.

It's exhausting just to read the list, but we weren't meant to live like this! We were created to travel through life with composure and calm. How is this possible? We have to learn to "think patience." Let me give you some examples:

WE HAVE TO LEARN TO "THINK PATIENCE."

When circumstances are uncontrollable—think patience.

So many things are beyond our control. Have you ever had to wait on a plane, been stuck in traffic or had a computer suddenly crash with a virus?

The New Testament writer, James, reminds us there is no occupation more unpredictable than that of a farmer. *"See how the farmer waits for the land to yield its valuable crop and how patient he is for the autumn and spring rains"* (James 5:7 NIV).

The farmer is at the mercy of the elements, waiting for two specific rains. First the *early* rain—when the seed is in the process of germination. Then the *late* rain which matures the seed and turns it into grain.

What an unreliable process! He prepares his land, plants his seed, and then has to wonder, "Will it rain? Will the bugs come? Will the hail storm destroy my crop? Will the market be up or down?" He has no control over these make-or-break factors.

Like the farmer, we need to exercise patience and allow God to do His mighty work.

When people seem unchangeable—think patience.

Have you ever tried to talk to someone about losing weight? It's a sensitive subject and not worth broaching too hastily.

> IT IS HUMAN NATURE TO RESIST CHANGE AND TO RESENT THOSE WHO THREATEN OUR COMFORT ZONE.

I know we function in a hurry-up world, but we need to realize transformation comes slowly. It is human nature to resist change and to resent those who threaten our comfort zone.

James points to the Old Testament prophets, who endured years of ridicule as they proclaimed God's message to their generation. *"Brothers, as an example of patience in the face of suffering, take the prophets who spoke in the name of the Lord"* (James 5:10 NIV).

When problems are unexplainable—think patience.

There are times when we face hurdles and can only ask "Why?" How many *good people* endure unexplainable circumstances such as:

- Not being able to have a child.
- Being passed over for a promotion you rightly deserved.
- Being laid off without notice or warning.

We live in a fallen world where there is sin and injustice. No one ever promised life would be fair. For this reason, it's vital to realistically face our unexplainable problems.

If you want to examine the life of someone who was nearly crushed by suffering, look at Job. In the words of James, *"Job is an example of a man who endured patiently. From his experience we see how the Lord's plan finally ended in good, for he is full of tenderness and mercy"* (James 5:11).

The Bible tells us Job was a wealthy man who had enormous resources of cattle, camel and sheep. He had servants and enjoyed a large family.

Job was also a devoted believer—*"He was blameless, a man of complete integrity. He feared God and stayed away from evil"* (Job 1:1).

131

One day, without explanation, in a period of about 48 hours, every one of his sons and daughters were murdered or kidnaped. All of his livestock were stolen or killed and his fields and buildings were burned.

In addition, he developed a very painful affliction.

The people around Job were perplexed as to why this adversity was happening. His friends arrived and said, "It's all your fault! What did you do to bring on this awful torment?"

> "IT'S ALL YOUR FAULT! WHAT DID YOU DO TO BRING ON THIS AWFUL TORMENT?"

His body became covered with a terrible case of boils from head to toe. In this painful condition, Job was sitting on an ash heap, scraping his skin with a piece of broken pottery, trying to get relief. His wife came to him and said, *"Curse God and die"* (Job 2:9).

Even though Job resented what was happening, he adamantly questioned conventional wisdom regarding *why* it was taking place. He agonized over the thought that perhaps God had forsaken him.

Yet, Job never lost faith in God. He declared, *"Though He slay me, yet will I trust Him"* (Job 13:15 NKJV).

An early church father remarked, "There may be a faith which never questions or complains, but greater still is a faith which is tortured by questions and still believes."

Job's trust was eventually rewarded. The Bible

records, *"...the Lord blessed Job in the second half of his life even more than in the beginning. For now he had fourteen thousand sheep, six thousand camels, one thousand teams of oxen, and one thousand female donkeys. He also gave Job seven more sons and three more daughters"* (Job 42:12-13).

After this, Job lived 140 more years, long enough to see four generations of his children and grandchildren. *"Then he died, an old man who had lived a long, good life"* (v.17).

GOD HAS HIS OWN TIMETABLE

We are always in a hurry for things to happen. For instance, we read of the soon return of Jesus and want Him to come immediately.

When you begin to study God's Word you find that scripture talks far more about the Second Coming of Christ than it does concerning His first arrival at Bethlehem. But here is what James tells us: *"...be patient and stand firm, because the Lord's coming is near"* (James 5:8 NIV).

History is moving toward this climactic moment and nothing—or anyone—is going to stop His triumphant return. The timetable is in God's hands, not ours. Scripture says, *"... no one knows the day or the hour when these things will happen, not even the angels in heaven or the Son himself. Only the Father knows"* (Matthew 24:35).

Until that hour, we are to occupy until He comes (Luke 19:13), diligently working at whatever task to which the Lord has called us. As Habakkuk wrote long ago, *"But these things I plan won't happen right away. Slowly, steadily, surely, the time approaches when the vision will be fulfilled. If it seems slow, do not despair, for these things will surely come to pass. Just be patient! They will not be overdue a single day!"* (Habakkuk 2:3 LB).

Since God has a purpose and a plan, we can be patient, knowing He is in complete control. At the end of the journey it will be worth the wait. Jesus says, *"Blessed are you when people insult you, persecute you and falsely say all kinds of evil against you because of me. Rejoice and be glad, because great is your reward in heaven"* (Matthew 5:11-12 NIV).

A "WAIT" GAINING STRATEGY

A little boy was standing at the foot of an escalator in a big department store intently watching the handrail. He never took his eyes off the black rubber handrail as the escalator kept going around and around. A curious salesperson saw him and finally asked, "Are you lost?"

The little fellow replied, "Nope. I'm just waiting for my chewing gum to come back!"

That determination is quite a contrast from people who become irritated and stressed when the world doesn't move as fast as they would like.

If you need to work on your PF—your Patience Factor—let me offer these suggestions:

1. Wait expectantly.

We don't bury a tulip bulb in the soil and see a beautiful flower pop up the next day. No, we wait for God's appointed season, springtime.

It is the same with the Father's pledge to us. What He says will come to pass. As David writes, *"That is why I wait expectantly, trusting God to help, for he has promised"* (Psalm 130:5 LB).

Why be in such a hurry? After all, *"It is dangerous and sinful to rush into the unknown"* (Proverbs 19:2 LB).

2. Develop a wider perspective.

You may have a top-notch resume and think you have great insight and creativity, yet these pale in comparison with what happens when you let God expand your horizons.

Stop for a moment and seek the Father's wisdom. *"Trust in the Lord with all your heart and lean not on your own understanding"* (Proverbs 3:5 NIV).

STOP FOR A MOMENT AND SEEK THE FATHER'S WISDOM.

You will be amazed with the results: *"'...for my*

135

thoughts are not your thoughts, neither are your ways my ways,' declares the Lord" (Isaiah 55:8 NIV).

3. Find a new way of looking at a situation—or a person.

Emotional and spiritual maturity is when you know the difference between "no" and "not yet," between denial and delay.

There's always more than one way to look at what's going on in your life. Exercise the patience to see people and events through new eyes.

Paul tells us what can happen when we are released from the past. He says, *"Now we can really serve God, not in the old way by obeying the letter of the law, but in the new way, by the Spirit"* (Romans 7:6).

4. Depend daily on God's power.

Don't rush to take matters into your own hands when the Lord has the strength to defeat the enemy and solve the problem. The great heros of scripture discovered this secret:

- Abraham *"waited patiently, and he received what God had promised"* (Hebrews 6:16).
- David said, *"I waited patiently for the Lord to help me, and he turned to me and heard my cry"* (Psalm 40:1).

136

- Solomon learned, *"It is better to be patient than powerful; it is better to have self-control than to conquer a city"* (Proverbs 16:32).
- Paul tells us, *"His glorious power will make you patient and strong enough to endure anything, and you will be truly happy"* (Colossians 1:11 CEV).

What glorious testimonies. Only God's power can make you patient and strong.

Ask the Lord to give you the patience of Job, the expectation of David and His strength to endure.

CHAPTER 15

THE UNEXPECTED CRISIS

Have no fear of sudden disaster...
for the Lord will be your confidence...
— PROVERBS 3:25-26

When friends sit around sharing their life experiences, many of their stories include phrases such as:

- "I was driving along, minding my own business, when..."
- "We were sound asleep when out of the blue...."
- "That telephone call totally changed my life."

Here is what we know about life's sudden emergencies:

139

Crises are unpreventable.

As long as you are breathing, get ready for "growing pains."

Perhaps you can identify with the psalmist as he writes, *"I am worn out from sobbing. Every night tears drench my bed; my pillow is wet from weeping. My vision is blurred by grief; my eyes are worn out because of all my enemies"* (Psalm 6:6-7).

It's not *if* you will face trouble, but *when.* God's Word says, *"My brethren, count it all joy when you fall into various trials..."* (James 1:2 NKJV).

Crises are inconstant.

Our difficulties are not always identical. They arrive in three different forms:

1. Some are *situational* in nature.

At times, external conditions occur which are much like Murphy's Law: Whatever can go wrong, will go wrong.

Solomon speaks of the moments, *"When calamity overcomes you like a storm, when you are engulfed by trouble, and when anguish and distress overwhelm you"* (Proverbs 1:27).

2. Some are *relational* in nature.

There's no getting away from "people problems."

Unfortunately, they often lead to strained relationships and shattered friendships.

In the words of David, *"I lie awake, lonely as a solitary bird on the roof. My enemies taunt me day after day. They mock and curse me"* (Psalm 102:7-8).

3. Some are emotional in nature.

If situations spiral out of our control, we are often overwhelmed by feelings—fear, guilt, worry or anger.

As Job described his emotions, *"My weary nights are filled with pain as though something were relentlessly gnawing at my bones"* (Job 30:16-17).

Crises are unbiased.

As a Christian you are not immune from difficulties. No matter how committed, the believer is subject to the same kinds of depression, disappointment and disease.

I've heard people remark, "Well, if you are in a mess it means you must have disobeyed God." This assumption simply isn't true.

> AS A CHRISTIAN YOU ARE NOT IMMUNE FROM DIFFICULTIES.

Jesus explains how God *"...gives his sunlight to both the evil and the good, and he sends rain on the just and on the unjust, too"* (Matthew 5:45).

You have a hidden resource. Although you may encounter the same trials as anyone else, there is a higher power at your disposal to deal with the issue. *"Though*

141

they stumble, they will not fall, for the Lord holds them by the hand" (Psalm 37:24).

Crises are unexpected.

Be prepared for the unpredictable!

_____ ❧ _____
BE PREPARED FOR THE UNPREDICTABLE!

Jesus was crossing the sea of Galilee with His disciples when, *"Without warning a furious storm came up..."* (Matthew 8:24 NIV).

Most crises happen unexpectedly; there's no advance notice.

"NOW WHAT?"

You may say, "Okay, I've feel like I've just been hit by a tsunami. Now what?"

The following is what has always worked for me:

Remember, I am not alone.

The reason we often want to run when the going gets tough is because we think we're all by ourselves.

When the storm arose, how quickly the disciples forgot, *"...he got into the boat"* (Matthew 8:23 NIV). Yes, Jesus was with them.

God spoke these words of comfort through the prophet Isaiah: *"Fear not, for I have redeemed you; I have summoned you by name; you are mine. When you pass through the waters, I will be with you; and when you pass through the rivers, they will not sweep over you"* (Isaiah 43:1-2 NIV).

It doesn't matter if the boat is rocking and the waters are choppy, as long as Christ is on board.

Acknowledge and accept that God cares.

When things go haywire, we often question God's concern—even His love. Nothing could be further from the truth. According to scripture His love is wider, greater and deeper then anything we can possibly fathom.

As the storm raged, *"Jesus was in the stern, sleeping on a cushion. The disciples woke him and said to him, 'Teacher, don't you care if we drown?'"* (Mark 4:38 NIV).

It was a natural reaction—one which has been repeated millions of times by those who feel abandoned: "Don't you care?"

Remember, Jesus said, *"Let us go over to the other side!"* (Mark 4:35 NIV). He had already assured the disciples a safe passage. They just needed to exercise their faith and depend on His presence.

The believer who places his total trust in the Almighty, can rest assured in this promise: He *"will not be overthrown by evil circumstances. God's constant care of him will make a deep impression on all who see it. He does not fear bad news, nor live in dread of what may happen. For he is settled in his mind that God will take care of him. That is why he is not afraid but can calmly face his foes"* (Psalm 112:6-8 LB).

Believe God is in charge.

The disciples worried unnecessarily because the Master was with them. Jesus, *"...got up, rebuked the wind and said to the waves, 'Quiet! Be still!' Then the wind died down and it was completely calm"* (Mark 4:39 NIV).

When you ask the Lord for safety and protection, let Him know, *"You are my defender and protector. You are my God; in you I trust.' He will keep you safe from all hidden dangers...you need not fear"* (Psalm 91:2-5 TEV).

Today, the Lord is telling you, "Let's go over to the other side!"

Just as fire gives light and rain makes a rainbow, let you crisis produce great expectations.

CHAPTER 16

NOTHING "JAZZY" ABOUT THE BLUES

While he himself went a day's journey into the desert.
He came to a broom tree, sat down under it and prayed
that he might die. "I have had enough, Lord," he said.
"Take my life; I am no better than my ancestors."
– 1 KINGS 19:4 NIV

Depression is a scourge which disrupts the lives of millions and causes tremendous emotional pain—not just for the person who is suffering, but for their family and friends.

It can come from any combination of biological, psychological and genetic factors.

Average people get depressed.

According to statistics, seventeen and a half million face depression each year in America. It affects those of all races, religions and economic backgrounds—and the problem becomes more severe with age.

Famous people get depressed.

"Black Dog" was Winston Churchill's name for his cloud of depression—which plagued him in his adult life. Tolstoy, author of *War and Peace*, suffered with such a psychological "darkness," he contemplated suicide. And Abraham Lincoln endured great bouts of despondency.

Godly people have been depressed.

Moses complained to the Lord, *"What did I do to deserve the burden of a people like this?...I'd rather you killed me than treat me like this"* (Numbers 11:11,15).

Jeremiah cried, *"Why then does my suffering continue? Why is my wound so incurable?"* (Jeremiah 15:18).

Job, at the lowest point of his travail, admitted, *"And now my heart is broken. Depression haunts my days"* (Job 30:16).

In other words, depression is *no respecter* of persons.

THE SHOWDOWN!

One of the most vivid accounts of dejection and despondency you will ever read is found in the life of the great prophet Elijah.

This Old Testament preacher was given the enormous task of standing before a corrupt king and giving him this message: "Because of your evil leadership, God is going to bring a drought on this land and it's not going to rain for years."

Of course, King Ahab and Queen Jezebel didn't appreciate those words, so Elijah had to go underground for his own safety.

During this time tension developed between the spokesman of the true God and the prophets of Baal—and soon there was a showdown.

> ELIJAH HAD TO GO UNDERGROUND FOR HIS OWN SAFETY.

Elijah suggested two altars should be constructed: "I'll build one to my God, and you build one to yours, and the one who responds by setting the altar on fire will be the one true God."

The 450 prophets of Baal prayed, cut themselves and cried out to their false god—and nothing happened.

Elijah then took water and poured it over his altar (and the wood under it) so there would be no suspicion of foul play. He prayed to God, and the Lord sent a fire from heaven and ignited the altar. The fire was so intense that even the water which was in the trough dried up.

Because His power had been soundly demonstrated, God signaled the drought was over.

Elijah looked in the heavens and said to King Ahab, "It's going to rain. You came here in your chariot; if you want to get back to Jezreel without getting bogged down, you'd better start now."

When Ahab left, the power of God fell on Elijah—so much so that he outran Ahab's chariot back to town. On the map that's a distance of approximately 18 miles!

147

But Elijah didn't have time to celebrate. Jezebel told him her husband was angry and that he'd better run for his life.

So flee is exactly what he did. Scripture tells us Elijah *"...went on alone into the desert, traveling all day. He sat down under a solitary broom tree and prayed that he might die. 'I have had enough, Lord,' he said. 'Take my life, for I am no better than my ancestors'"* (1 Kings 19:4).

YOUR ESCAPE

An interesting finding of research is that depression is not the result of laziness, lack of will power, personal failure or weakness. It is a treatable disease.

If you are despondent and are looking for relief, let me offer theses suggestions:

Recognize the contributing factors.

There are moments we are more vulnerable to the dark days of depression than others. What causes the problem to worsen?

Physical fatigue.

When Elijah fell into depression, he was exhausted. After all, he had just run 18 miles, plus walked a day's journey into the desert.

Constant stress.

The prophet had to "face down" a national leader, plus confront 450 false prophets. That had to be a tough task.

Stop exaggerating the past.

Certainly there were problems in Elijah's life, but he didn't need to dwell on them.

Instead of laying under a tree, asking God to take his life, Elijah should have rejoiced over the miracles the Lord had already performed.

- He was fed by ravens (1 Kings 17:4-7).
- In a drought, God multiplied the widow's mite, and they both were fed (1 Kings 17:8-16).
- On Mount Carmel, God showed himself strong and demonstrated His power in a tremendous way (1 Kings 18:24-38).

Why magnify the misery of your past when there is so much for which you can be thankful? Say with the psalmist, *"Praise the Lord, O my soul, and forget not all his benefits"* (Psalm 103:2 NIV).

Allow gratitude to change your attitude.

I love the words of the old hymn, "Count your blessings, name them one by one.

WHY MAGNIFY THE MISERY OF YOUR PAST WHEN THERE IS SO MUCH FOR WHICH YOU CAN BE THANKFUL?

149

And it will surprise you what the Lord has done."

Do the "right stuff" now.

There are actions you can take which will help lift your spirits.

Physical renewal.

Elijah took time out and rested. The Bible records he *"lay down and slept under the broom tree"* (1 Kings 19:5).

> IF YOU ARE A "TYPE A" PERSONALITY, LET ME REMIND YOU IT'S OKAY TO SLOW DOWN AND RECOUP.

If you are a "Type A" personality, let me remind you it's okay to slow down and recoup. To some people, staying busy is like holding a wolf by its ears. We don't want to, but we're afraid of what will happen if we let go!

God sent angels to Elijah who said, *"'Get up and eat!' He looked around and saw some bread baked on hot stones and a jar of water!"* (vv.7-7). After a second miracle meal, the prophet was physically renewed and *"the food gave him enough strength to travel forty days and forty nights to Mount Sinai, the mountain of God"* (v.8).

Spiritual renewal.

Hiding in a deep, damp cave on Mount Sinai, Elijah

reconnected with God. A voice told him to *"Go out and stand on the mountain in the presence of the Lord, for the Lord is about to pass by"* (v.11).

There was a powerful wind, then an earthquake, then fire, yet God did not speak to Elijah through any of these calamities. His spiritual renewal came when he heard the Lord speak in a *"still small voice"* (v.12 NKJV).

Relational renewal.

During his depression, Elijah moaned to the Lord how there was no one who understood what he was going through. Now with his passion rekindled, the prophet was led to a young man named Elisha, who was plowing in a field. He became the prophet's assistant and there was now a dynamic duo—a powerful relationship for God's Kingdom (vv.19-21).

Purpose renewal.

Elijah got back in the game. He rediscovered his purpose and followed the Lord's plan for his future (vv 15-18).

Friend, you are never so broken or too "down" to offer yourself to the Lord. No matter how little you think you possess, you'll be amazed what the Lord can do.

Allow God's promises to produce optimism.

I enjoyed hearing the story of a young man at a football game who turned to the gentleman seated next to him and asked, "Excuse me sir, can you tell me what time it is?"

When the elder man didn't respond, he thought, "Maybe he's hard of hearing," so he spoke a little louder, "Excuse me sir, can you tell me what time it is?"

Again, total silence. So finally, he tapped the gentleman on the shoulder and said, "Sir, I was hoping you could tell me the time. Have I offended you in some way?"

The older man finally responded, "Yes, as a matter of fact you have, because I know how this conversation is going to progress. You're going to ask me what time it is and I'll tell you. Then we'll start talking about our families and we will become friends. I'll invite you to my house and you'll meet my daughter. The two of you will fall in love and get married. And frankly, I don't want a son-in-law who can't afford a watch!"

What pessimism!

I know it's a challenge to remain positive when you're feeling alone and depressed, but think of the alternative!

God's Word is filled with hope and positive encouragement for your soul. When you read it every day you will begin to see the dark cloud of despair disappear.

Break apart from busyness.

Perhaps it's time to start trimming your schedule. Why? Because, *"...being too busy gives you nightmares"* (Ecclesiastes 5:3).

Saying "Yes" to every request can overwhelm you and lead to tremendous stress and pressure. It's much better to give yourself some time and say, "Let me get back to you."

The Bible says, *"Teach us to number our days and recognize how few they are; help us to spend them as we should"* (Psalm 90:12 LB).

Don't over-commit to your schedule. Give yourself time to breathe!

THE STRENGTH OF YOUR HEART

If you are among the millions affected by depression, search for the causes, not the symptoms—and base your life on truth, not feelings.

Most important, let God speak to you through His Word. As the psalmist discovered, *"My flesh and my heart may fail, but God is the strength of my heart and my portion forever"* (Psalm 73:26 NIV).

**Just as night turns into day,
the dark clouds of your life will lift and
vanish in the light of God's love.**

153

CHAPTER 17

THE HOMECOMING

...his father said to the servants, "Quick!
Bring the finest robe in the house and put it
on him. Get a ring for his finger, and sandals for his
feet. And kill the calf we have been fattening in the pen.
We must celebrate with a feast, for this son of mine
was dead and has now returned to life. He was lost,
but now he is found." So the party began.
– LUKE 15:22-24

Jesus tells us the story of a young man who chose to ask for his inheritance early—determined to leave his father's house and live the "good life."

On his adventure, the prodigal son made one misstep after another, wasting his money on wild living. Now hungry and broke, he had sunk to feeding pigs!

It's easy to criticize the young man; however, at the lowest point of his runaway life he made a monumental decision. In the parable, we are told, *"When he finally came to his senses, he said to himself, 'At home even the hired men have food enough to spare, and here I am, dying of hunger! I will go home to my father and say, "Father, I have sinned against both heaven and you, and I am no longer worthy of being called your son. Please take me on as a hired man"* (Luke 15-17-19).

The remorseful son began the long trek home, not knowing how he would be received. Then, while he was still a great distance away, *"his father saw him coming. Filled with love and compassion, he ran to his son, embraced him, and kissed him."* (v.20).

It was the start of a homecoming celebration!

THERE IS HOPE

Perhaps there have been times when you were at the end of your rope, ready to throw up your hands and say, "I quit! Life isn't worth living!" A feeling of brokenness may have invaded your soul, as if you were being trampled down or crushed in spirit. You find yourself using words such as "survive," "endure" or "just make it through" to describe your days and nights.

Just as the father in this parable rejoiced at his son's return, your Heavenly Father is watching and waiting for you—longing to bless and renew your life.

Jesus came to "bind up" our wounds. He offers His personal attention to your needs—soothing the pain and restoring you to health and wholeness.

God will intervene in miraculous ways, giving you the hope and confidence you need. You will be able to say with Paul, *"I can do everything with the help of Christ who gives me the strength I need"* (Philippians 4:13).

I love the words penned by Stephen Curtis Chapman: "His strength is perfect when our strength is gone. He'll carry us when we can't carry on. Raised in His power, the weak become strong. His strength is perfect."

It is my prayer you will take the timeless principles we have shared and apply them. The Lord will fill you with His power to live above the emotional undercurrents that threaten to drag you down and pull you away.

It's time to stop running.

God is waiting with open arms for you.

For a Complete List of Resources or to
Schedule the Author for Speaking Engagements,
Contact:

Tom Smiley
4015 Soapstone Lane
Gainesville, GA 30506

Phone: 770-536-0843   770 532-6307
Fax: 770-532-6308
Email: tsmiley@lakewood-baptist.com
tsmiles55@gmail.com
Internet: www.lifewithsmiles.com